Teaching Writing

Explorations in Language Study

Explorations in Language Study
General Editors
Peter Doughty   Geoffrey Thornton

TEACHING WRITING: THE DEVELOPMENT OF WRITTEN LANGUAGE SKILLS

Geoffrey Thornton

EDWARD ARNOLD

© Geoffrey Thornton 1980
First published 1980
by Edward Arnold (publishers) Ltd
41 Bedford Square, London WC1B 3DQ

British Library Cataloguing in Publication Data

Thornton, Geoffrey
   Teaching writing. — (Explorations in language study).
   1. Language arts — Great Britain
   2. Authorship — Study and teaching — Great Britain
   I. Title   II. Series
   808'.042'07   LB1575.8

ISBN 0-7131-6282-1

Printed in Great Britain by
Richard Clay (The Chaucer Press) Ltd,
Bungay, Suffolk

General Introduction

In the course of our efforts to develop a linguistic focus for work in English language, which was published as *Language in Use*, we came to realize the extent of the growing interest in what we would call a linguistic approach to language. Lecturers in Colleges and Departments of Education see the relevance of such an approach in the education of teachers. Many teachers in schools and in Colleges of Further Education recognize that 'educational failure is primarily *linguistic* failure', and are turning to Linguistic Science for some kind of exploration and practical guidance. Many of those now exploring the problems of relationships, community or society, from a sociological or psychological point of view wish to make use of a linguistic approach to the language in so far as it is relevant to these problems.

We were conscious of the wide divergence between the aims of the linguist, primarily interested in describing language as a system for organizing 'meanings', and the needs of those who now wanted to gain access to the insights that resulted from that interest. In particular, we were aware of the wide gap that separated the literature of academic Linguistics from the majority of those who wished to find out what Linguistic Science might have to say about language and the use of language.

Out of this experience emerged our own view of that much-used term, 'Language Study', developed initially in the chapters of *Exploring Language*, and now given expression in this series. Language Study is not a subject, but a process, which is why the series is called *Explorations in Language Study*. Each exploration is focused upon a meeting point between the insights of Linguistic Science, often in conjunction with other social sciences, and the linguistic questions raised by the study of a particular aspect of

1

individual behaviour or human society.

The volumes in the series have a particular relevance to the role of language in teaching and learning. The editors intend that they should make a basic contribution to the literature of Language Study, doing justice equally to the findings of the academic disciplines involved and the practical needs of those who now want to take a linguistic view of their own particular problems of language and the use of language.

Peter Doughty
Geoffrey Thornton

Contents

Acknowledgements

I should like to acknowledge the contribution made to this book by my friends and colleagues (the terms are interchangeable) in the Cheshire Adult Literacy Project from 1975 – 77; by those who were good enough to read and comment on it in draft, Peter Doughty, John Keen and John Welch; and by all those with whom I have had the pleasure of discussing the issues raised in the book, especially Martin Chilcott, Stephen Eyers, John Richmond and Jim Wight.

Geoffrey Thornton

1 Introductory

The main source of inspiration for this book was the Adult Literacy Project in Cheshire, with which I was closely involved from 1975 – 77. Like all Local Education Authorities in England, Cheshire responded to the initiative taken by the BBC in 1974, when they began to prepare programmes for Adult Non-readers. Since there were insufficient resources to set up a system of paid tutors to meet the needs of the many students who were expected to ask for help, it was decided to recruit and train volunteer tutors. These came forward in large enough numbers to meet the demand. The majority were men and women who had had no training for, or experience of, teaching. They were given a twelve-hour introductory course before being paired with a student, initially on a one-to-one basis. As the students made the 'break-through to literacy', they moved into small groups of five or six.

These students, well over a thousand in Cheshire by the end of 1976, were of all ages from sixteen to eighty-six. Detailed analysis , published in *Education in Cheshire*,[1] revealed that 32 per cent were in their twenties, 22 per cent in their thirties, and 14 per cent in their forties. How far these percentages reflect the numbers of adult non-readers in the population of England as a whole we cannot know. What we do know, however, is that willingness to come forward and ask for help is related to need, and need is liable to be greater in one's twenties and thirties, when marriage, family and job may create urgent demands for the benefits of literacy, than in one's forties and fifties, when one has been living with the presence of the handicap for so long.

Nevertheless, the students in their fifties and sixties, even seventies and eighties, demonstrated clearly that, despite the impression sometimes given in the press and elsewhere, it has always been the

5

case that some pupils have come through the school system of their time either without learning to read and write at all, or with the ability insufficiently established to survive into adult life. Now, many years after they had left school, they were being given the opportunity to repair this omission, an opportunity of which, in the vast majority of cases, they took successful advantage. Part-time volunteer tutors succeeded where school had failed. Why?

The usual answer given to this question is 'the one-to-one relationship'. Certainly, this is important. The tutor can give undivided attention to the student, can analyse his or her needs, can diagnose strengths and weaknesses, can decide on relevant methods and devise appropriate materials.

Given the motivation of the student, there is here a good recipe for success. But if success does not come, the Adult Literacy Tutor will change the approach. It is very difficult, when you are seeing a student for a weekly session in a one-to-one situation, to persist for long with teaching methods that are not working. Yet this is what happens in school. Methods purporting to teach children how to learn to write are persisted with in junior schools, and throughout the years in secondary school, despite the evidence in the writing of the pupils that the methods are not working.

This constitutes the crucial difference between the approach adopted by the Adult Literacy Tutor and the approach adopted in many schools. The former teaches for success, and, if success does not come, then the method is changed. In school the approach is through methods hallowed by tradition, reproduced in generation after generation of course books, seemingly impervious to change in the light of insights afforded by the work done in the last twenty-five years on the relationship between language and learning.

When these methods do not work, blame for failure is made to rest with the pupil instead of with the method. But pupils who have failed, or been failed, in school are now succeeding through the efforts of the Adult Literacy Project. No longer can we afford to say, of any pupil, 'he can't' or 'she will never'.

This book, then, rests upon the conviction that it is possible to do more by way of teaching pupils to write effectively in schools, both primary and secondary, than has hitherto been the case. If it owes much to the Cheshire Adult Literacy Project, it also owes a debt to the late Mina Shaughnessy's book, *Errors and Expectations*,[2] which was written out of her experience with students at City College, New York. Some students, that is; those who, towards the end of the sixties, began to enter colleges like City College, although they 'were not by traditional standards ready for college'. Of these, Mrs Shaughnessy says, some

> had been left so far behind the others in their formal education that they appeared to have little chance of catching up, students whose difficulties with the written language seemed of a different order . . . as if they had come, you might say, from a different country, or at least through different schools, where even very modest standards of high-school literacy had not been met.

The reaction of some of her colleagues was interesting.

> Not uncommonly, teachers announced to their supervisors (or even their students) after only a week of class that everyone was probably going to fail. These were students, they insisted, whose problems at this stage were irremediable.

These were teachers of English, telling their students, after only a week in class, that they were going to fail. One wonders what perception of their role as teachers they had that would enable them so to confess their own incompetence, or indeed what equipment they had been given as English teachers that had left them so inadequately equipped to meet their students' needs.

But this attitude towards the quality of the pupils' writing is not uncommon amongst teachers, including English teachers. It is neatly exemplified in Denys Thompson's introduction to Sir Alec Clegg's *The Excitement of Writing*. After a devastating attack on much of the traditional content of English as a school subject, he then writes:

> Mechanical accuracy in the writing of English, for example, will come or will not come, with maturity, and there is very little that teacher or text-book can do about it.[3]

There is a disturbing fatalism about this, which has the effect of absolving teachers from their professional responsibility. They do their best, of course, but some pupils seem to be beyond help. At least, of the kind that is traditionally offered.

The concern of Sir Alec Clegg's book, and of almost all of the many books about writing in school published in the last twenty years, notably those deriving from the work of James Britton and his colleagues at the London Institute of Education,[4] has been essentially with the act of writing as a psychological process. The effect has been to encourage teachers to be much more sensitive in stimulating and responding to childrens' writing. But their influence has stopped short of showing teachers how they can help their pupils to gain greater mastery of the writing system itself. In the same way, W. R. Harpin, who, in *The Second 'R'*, sets his discussion of the place of writing in schools today in the context of a historical review of changing attitudes, can list as the sixth of his 'unanswered questions' in the last chapter,

> What effective ways are there of helping the non-progressing child through his difficulties?[5]

It is high time that we began to answer that question. We have accomplished in English education in the last thirty years an institutional revolution: the majority of eleven-year-olds now go to Comprehensive Schools, instead of being sorted, twenty-odd per cent to Grammar Schools, the rest to Secondary Moderns. What we have not yet accomplished is a pedagogic revolution, which will bring better teaching methods to the task of ensuring that the Comprehensive School will give to its pupils the full educational benefits that it undoubtedly can. Nowhere is this more important than in the case of writing, for it is by their ability to write that pupils will, in the end, succeed or fail in the educational system. The most significant judgments are made in written examinations. If we help pupils to write better, we help them to success within the educational system.

2 Language in our heads

If only they could write as well as they can talk.

This is a comment not infrequently heard in schools. It even appears on school reports and suggests a surprising degree of detachment from the learning process on the part of teachers who make it.

Anyone who can 'talk well' possesses a vast knowledge of language, the sort of knowledge which enables any speaker of any language to put together sounds in stretches of language which convey meaning to others, and to listen to, and take meaning from, the speech of others. As Courtney Cazden put it in *Child Language and Education*,

> Language is knowledge in our heads; speech is the realization of that knowledge in behaviour[1].

As with speech, so with writing, which is, as pointed out in *The Development of Writing Abilities*, another form of behaviour dependent upon the knowledge of language we have in our heads.

> Language is knowledge in our heads; writing is a realization of that knowledge in behaviour.

Acquiring the ability to write is the exercise of a biological capability, an extension of the ability to speak which is a characteristic of the human species. Underlying the ability to do both is the capacity of the human brain to acquire and store knowledge about language, and enable that knowledge to be drawn upon to put language to use. This book asks why, in schools in a literate society, some children are able to draw upon their internalized knowledge

9

of language and learn to write with comparative ease, while some seem unable. That, with the exception of those born with defective brains, they can do it is beyond doubt. The Adult Literacy Project, if it has proved nothing else, has proved that. What comes between knowledge of language in the head and its realization in writing?

We start from the proposition that all normal youngsters will possess, by the time they enter school at five, an extensive knowledge of language in their heads, and a well-developed ability to use it in the speech of their mother-tongue.

This language, and how to use it, has been learnt as part of the process of growing up in the environment into which they have been born, usually a small community like a family. It will thus be the language of that community, or more properly, the version of that language that individuals make for themselves from the language they hear around them.

What the children develop for themselves is the ability to use language to make meaning, to construct meaningful utterances. This entails learning the sound system of the language, how to put sounds together to make words, and how to put words together to make meaning. In the process, knowledge is acquired about language, especially what it is used for, what it can be used for, and when and how it is appropriate to use it. This is knowledge at an intuitive level, gained from the direct, first-hand experience of language as it is used in the face-to-face situations of early life, and learning it has required virtually no direct, explicit teaching beyond the repetition, by the parents, of what they sense that the child may be trying to say. You do not need to be taught Parts of Speech in the cradle in order to learn to speak!

What youngsters bring with them into school at the age of five is language as a going concern, which enables them to function linguistically in the environment in which they have grown up. This means that they possess a linguistic system, the framework of which they have acquired, as M.A.K. Halliday insists, by the age of two and a half, and a knowledge of how to deploy that system in the real-life situations of which they have had experience.[2] They will now have to extend this knowledge in order to enable them to function at school, to work with new people in new situations, and, above all, to become literate. Being literate is here taken to mean possessing the ability to switch from spoken language to written language freely and at will, in response to need. This implies possession of the judgment required to determine need, and of requisite mastery of the writing system. Learning to read and write does not require the learner to have an explicit understanding of the processes involved. The pupils in the reception class in any Infant School will demonstrate this as they begin to find visual correspondences for the language in their heads. The difficulties which confront them will be of two orders. They are (1) those inherent in transposing a sound system into a visual system, and (2) those which derive from mistaken views of the nature of the process held by those who teach them, and those members of the public (e.g. parents and politicians) who exert pressure on teachers.

Language, then, is primarily a system of sounds used in face-to-face situations with other people, where features other than language, like expression and gesture, can be employed in consort with language in order to tie the language to the context and to make and convey meaning. If a speaker does not succeed in conveying his intended meaning, he can try again. He can do this at any stage of his utterance, going back to the beginning before he is halfway through, altering, amending, saying a crucial bit in two or three different ways. In normal conversation, the only record of an utterance is in the brain of the listener, the only criterion of a successful utterance that the listener should be able to make meaning from it. The utterance will consist typically of groups of words carrying bits of meaning which add up to the totality of meaning that the speaker is seeking to convey, and will include the um's and er's and pauses which are a feature of all spontaneous speech.

The writer does not face his reader as the speaker ordinarily faces his audience. He faces a piece of paper that will be read in another place at some future time. A speaker can alter, cancel, start again. A writer can do this at the drafting stage, but at some point he must let go of his writing, and, once he has, he can do nothing to alter what he has written. It stands, or falls, by itself. It is not, like spontaneous speech, inextricably bound to the context in which it occurs. The writer is unable to make use of all those devices, gestures, tone of voice, intonation, repetition, to which the speaker can resort, in the presence of his audience and the immediacy of his context. As Abercrombie says,

> The whole object of written language is to be free of any immediate context . . . .[3]

The writer has to construct his own context, and attempt to

11

reach his audience not by making sounds in the air but by making marks on paper, arranged according to the conventions of the writing system he is using. The way in which he organizes his writing is therefore of the utmost significance, because the way in which the reader will read it is determined by the way in which the writer has written it. It is a commonplace experience, for example, that a typewritten communication, however poorly put together, is likely to carry more weight than a handwritten. In English, the marks have to be arranged in horizontal lines from left to right. Other languages have other conventions. Arabic, for instance, goes from right to left, horizontally, Chinese from top to bottom vertically. Spaces are left between words, although the erratic use of hyphens demonstrates that in some cases there is no unanimity as to what exactly constitutes a word, e.g. full stop or full-stop.

The words, which are made up of letters, have to be arranged into sentences, whereas words in speech are sequenced in groups which do not always aspire to be sentences. Sentences are demarcated by full stops and capital letters, while other punctuation marks occur within sentences.

Convention governs other aspects of writing, besides spelling and punctuation. The most important are to do with what kind of language is thought to be *appropriate* for writing down; many features of spoken language — words, phrases, slang expressions — are not considered appropriate for transfer to the written mode. This confronts many youngsters not only with the task of discovering which features of their own language are not appropriate to many of the varieties of written English the curriculum demands of them, but also of learning more suitable equivalents which may lie outside the range of the language in their heads. This is one of the reasons which led Sartre to remark, in *Les Mots*, 'on parle dans sa propre langue, on écrit en langue étrangère'.[4]

Sartre was summing up the difficulties inherent in the effort of transposing language from the spoken medium to the written. His choice of words, however, illuminates an especial difficulty confronting some of the children at present in our schools.

For them, the business of learning to write is literally the business of learning to write in a foreign language, since they are not native speakers of English. Such children come into our schools at all ages, bringing with them a variety of different languages. In 1978, ten per cent of the pupils in Inner London primary and secondary schools spoke between them a total of 128 different languages as their mother tongues. They may already be literate in their own language, and have some mastery of a writing system very different from English. For them, learning to write in English is learning to write in a foreign language. This book is not principally about their predicament.

There is, however, another category of pupil which is very much the concern of the book — the pupil who speaks, as his inherited language, a dialect of English other than the dialect known as Standard English, which is defined by Hughes and Trudgill in *English Accents and Dialects* as:

> the dialect of educated people throughout the British Isles. It is the dialect normally used in writing, for teaching in schools and universities, and heard on radio and television.[5]

For the purposes of the argument *at this point*, it does not matter whether the dialect in question is an English regional dialect, as spoken for example in Birmingham or Norfolk, or a dialect of English originating outside the British Isles, say, in the West Indies.

The difficulty may be illustrated by looking closely at a question asked by an Art teacher in a London school, 'What do you do', he said, 'about the pupil who says in class, "Cezanne didn't have no ruler, did he?" ' The concern was not, as it happens, with what the pupil ought to be writing, but with what he ought to be saying. Nevertheless, in this instance, the principle is the same.

What the teacher was really asking was something like, 'What ought I to do about a pupil who uses a double negative?' 'Double negative' is the term usually applied to the linguistic device of producing a negative statement by negating more than one word in a sentence, 'Cezanne did*n't* have *no* ruler,' instead of negating one word, as in 'Cezanne did not have a ruler' or 'Cezanne had no ruler.' This so-called 'double negative' (more than two negatives can occur, as in, 'You won't never smell nothing') is a common feature of many English dialects. In fact, as Hughes and Trudgill say in *English Accents and Dialects*,

> It is safe to say that constructions of the type, 'I didn't have no dinner' are employed by a majority of English speakers.[6]

However, in Standard English, and thus in writing, it is usual to negate only one word.

That the teacher should ask what he should do about the pupil's double negative in the spoken language suggests that he thought its use was evidence of an 'inferior' dialect, an example of 'bad grammar', or simply 'wrong', despite the fact that there was no ambiguity or lack of clarity in what the pupil had said; despite the fact, in other words, that as a bit of language, 'Cezanne didn't have no ruler' worked perfectly well in conveying the meaning intended.

In Chapter 2 of their book, Hughes and Trudgill give a dozen examples of grammatical differences between Standard English and non-standard dialects. They start with 'multiple negation', and include other common features like variant present tense forms (e.g. 'She like him' for 'She likes him'); relative pronouns (e.g. 'That was the man what done it'); adverbs and adjectives (e.g. 'He ran quick' for 'He ran quickly'); and the past tense of irregular verbs.

Many, perhaps the majority, of youngsters entering infant schools as native speakers of a dialect of English will have some, or most, of these features as part of their habitual way of speaking. If they are to learn to write appropriately, they must add to their store of language the forms required by Standard English.

All use of language involves choice. The more language one has, the more choice one has. Moreover, the notion that language involves choice, at least at one level, is usually learnt very early, probably when someone says to you something like, 'You mustn't speak to granny like that.' Such experiences give an early understanding of the twin concepts of choice and appropriacy, although in practice understanding is not enough. You must be able to choose to be appropriate. You must be able to choose to write 'I saw him', even though you habitually say 'I seen him'. You must be able to choose to write, 'Cezanne did not have a ruler', even if you ordinarily say 'Cezanne didn't have no ruler'.

You must be able to choose. You must have the linguistic means at your disposal, and you must want to say 'I saw him'. It is at this stage that it helps to make intuitive knowledge explicit, to raise the intuitive understanding of the concepts of choice and appropriacy that all native speakers of a language have to a conscious level. It is at this stage, however, that any misconceptions about language held by the teacher may get in the way. It has been suggested that the teacher who asked, 'What should we do about the pupil who says, "Cezanne didn't have no ruler?" ' thought that this was 'wrong' or 'bad grammar'. He was, in effect, asking, 'What can we do to replace this bad grammar by good?' If he then proceeded to tell the pupil that what he had said was 'wrong' and that he *ought* to say instead 'Cezanne had no ruler', the pupil might be forgiven for being a little puzzled. How could a way of saying something that was the normal way amongst those that he had been talking to for fourteen years, and was perfectly intelligible to everybody, be 'wrong'? To try to get him to agree is tantamount to asking him to betray his background, with which his language is so intimately bound up. On the basis of such misunderstanding, the chance of the pupil learning anything is slight.

If, however, we start from what he already knows, not so much about linguistic forms but about linguistic usage, we may have a chance. He knows, certainly by the age of fourteen, that he doesn't speak to his parents as he speaks to his brothers and sisters, or to his teachers as he speaks to his peers out of school. On this knowledge may be built an understanding of the need to write in ways that may differ from speech. Given the understanding, and the will, the difference between 'Cezanne didn't have no ruler' and 'Cezanne had no ruler' is reduced to manageable proportions.

In his well known paper, 'The logic of non-standard English', W. B. Labov examines the notion that the Black American dialects are linguistically inferior to White American dialects, and by their very impoverishment provide an insufficient vehicle for learning. He concludes, 'There is no reason to believe that any non-standard vernacular is in itself an obstacle to learning. The chief problem is ignorance of language on the part of all concerned.'[7]

It is a conclusion which points to the need for all teachers to understand what language is, and how it works. It is a conclusion which underlines the plea contained in the Bullock Report for a substantial element of language study to be included in the training of all teachers. For, so long as the intellectual equipment of teachers contains a view of language that is, in linguistic terms, essentially pre-Copernican, then for so long will substantial numbers of pupils in our schools fail to realize their potential. Teachers who cannot bring a proper linguistic perspective to bear on a scrutiny of what they are doing in the classroom cannot, in the end, enable pupils to get the language in their heads on to paper to the best advantage.

3 Behaviour on paper

I can put it into words, but I can't put it on paper.

Speech consists of sounds made by the mouth, writing of marks made by the hand, or even, as J.Z. Young notes in *Programs of the Brain*, 'by moving the head, or indeed with the big toe.'[1] Writing represents visually the sounds of language, a development that followed speech in the history of human language, just as it follows the acquisition of speech in the lives of those of us who become literate. While nearly every human being can speak, by no means every human being can write, for many languages do not possess writing systems. In those societies which have developed writing systems, it is observable that the written language tends to acquire a status which elevates it above the spoken language as a form of communication. Some people, in fact, believe that speech is a corrupt form of writing (what happens when you speak a language that has no written form to corrupt?), and that words should be 'pronounced as they are spelt'.

Speech and writing are manifestations of the same phenomenon. Children already have expertise in the one when they come to school. The task of the teacher is to help them invest that expertise in acquiring mastery of the other, and to do that teachers need to understand the relationship between speech and writing, the similarities and the differences. For the pupil, the most significant difference between them is that his success, or failure, in the educational system will rest, ultimately, on his ability to write. To put it at its crudest, on his ability to do well in written examinations.

When language has been committed to paper in the form of writing, there is a permanence about it not ordinarily associated with speech. (The invention and development of the tape-recorder has necessitated the use of the word 'ordinarily' in the preceding sentence. Watergate has taught us, if nothing else, that speech can sometimes acquire a kind of permanence.) But the intention behind committing yourself to paper is that the end-product shall continue to exist beyond the moment when you have decided that the pen can leave the paper. This has advantages and drawbacks. On the one hand, you can, in theory at least, work on it for as long as you like, or as long as you are allowed, drafting and re-drafting, working and re-working, editing and polishing. On the other hand, it means that once you let go of the paper it is possible for judgments to be made on what you have written, by anyone who wishes to read what you have written. Some will have particular reasons for reading what you have written, like the reviewers who will review this book, or the literary critics who read poems, or employers who read applications for a job, or examiners who read examination papers.

This is not to deny that judgments will sometimes be made on the way in which one speaks. Others will comment, from time to time, on one's accent, on one's choice of words, on one's seeming inability to answer a question, and so on. There will be times when, for a candidate at an interview, for a politician making a speech, for a participant in a Public Speaking Competition, the judgments of others about one's performance will have important consequences. But the fact remains that, for the pupils during their eleven years of statutory education in the United Kingdom, it is on their ability to write that judgments with the most important consequences will be made. On these judgments will rest, for example, their chances of proceeding to some form of Higher or Further Education. It would appear, therefore, that mastery of the writing system is the greatest gift that schools can bestow on those who pass through them.

What, precisely, does 'mastery of the writing system' involve? In *The Development of Writing Abilities*, there occurs this sentence:

> In putting the finishing touches to any piece of writing, one becomes aware, once again, of the twofold nature of the whole process — the need to meet demands and satisfy the reader, and the need of the writer to satisfy himself, to do what he wanted to do.[2]

This sums up neatly the predicament the writer finds himself in when faced with the need to write — how to 'meet demands and satisfy the reader' and, at the same time, how 'to satisfy himself'.

Of course, before one can find oneself in this position one must have some qualifications. One must be able to evaluate the nature of the demands being made, to know — in some sense — what *will* 'satisfy the reader', and one must have acquired sufficient mastery of the writing system to be able to meet those demands. Why use a phrase like 'mastery of the writing system?' Why not simply say something like 'must be able to write well enough'? The introduction of the term 'writing system' is not intended as pedantry, but as an attempt to emphasize the complexity of the process, a complexity not sufficiently recognized by those who regard writing as just a matter of spelling and punctuation. Writing *is* a matter of spelling and punctuation, but is much more than that.

At the heart of the writing system are the correspondences between the sounds of the language and the symbols that represent them on the page. There must be some agreement about these correspondences, or there would be no possibility of reading and understanding what somebody else had written. It is now widely believed that there is a transcendent value attaching to the correspondences which have become established in English, and that the ability to spell orthographically is the hallmark of the educated man. It was not always the case. Before the publication of Johnson's Dictionary in 1755 provided a universally acknowledged reference book, variations in the spelling of words were acceptable, provided those variations were within the limits of mutual understanding, although five years before this Lord Chesterfield had written to his son, 'I must tell you that orthography, in the true sense of the word, is so absolutely necessary for a man of letters, or a gentleman, that one false spelling may bring ridicule upon him for the rest of his life.' Even today, there are words (e.g. jewellery/jewelry, judgment/judgement) for which even the most prestigious dictionaries list variant spellings. Nevertheless a writer will need to take into account the reader's expectations about the merit of spelling a word in one way rather than another. It is part of the argument of the book that, if it is possible for a writer to use 'inshoerance' as a correspondence, then it is possible, and just as easy, for him to learn that 'insurance' is the preferred correspondence. (See p. 48.)

Likewise with punctuation. One of the strongest conventions governing the way in which we put language on paper is that sentences should begin with a capital letter and end with a full stop. It is sometimes said that, unless one does this, the reader will not be able to understand what one has written. There is only one answer to that. It begins,

> Yes because he never did a thing like that before as ask to get his
> breakfast in bed with a couple of eggs . . .

and goes on for 46 pages. It is, of course, Molly Bloom's stream of consciousness that ends James Joyce's *Ulysses*. It is not unintelligible, although it demands closer attention from the reader than usual. Joyce has exploited his mastery of the writing system in order to produce a particular effect. He has done it by defying the convention that demands capital letters and full stops to mark off sentences. Unless they are striving for a similar effect in a context that allows it, most writers need to take into account the expectation in their readers that they will follow this convention. Unless you are James Joyce, you run the risk of being thought less than literate if you do not use full stops.

Mastery of the writing system, then, does involve the ability to spell and punctuate in a way that satisfies the expectations of the reader. If we can distinguish between *how* one tries to put on paper *what* one wants to mean, then some grasp of spelling and punctuation is necessary to the *how*. Mina Shaughnessy uses this distinction when pointing out the danger for the writer whose reader is preoccupied with what he considers to be errors of spelling and punctuation.

> . . . they shift the reader's attention from where he is going
> (meaning) to how he is getting there (code).[3]

That is, they divert attention from the meaning of the writing to the means that are being employed to convey the meaning. But before a reader can be in this position at all, it is the writer who must know where he is going. Moreover, if he is to stand a reasonable chance of arriving successfully at the end of his journey, his mastery of the writing system will need to extend beyond spelling and punctuation.

How far his mastery will need to extend will depend upon the journey he is making, and his reason for making it. We know the purposes for which writing is used in a literate society, we see the evidence all around us, but why, at any given time, should an individual decide to write? Presumably because he acknowledges the need. If this be so, then he is motivated to write. He knows who he wants to write to, and why, or, in the now familiar terms, he perceives the function of the writing, and the audience for which it is intended. He knows where he wants to go, but how does he get there?

By putting words on paper. Which words? Words that he hopes will convey his meaning to his intended audience. If he does succeed in putting together meaningful assemblies of words, we can take it for granted that such assemblies will be grammatical. Language that works, that conveys meaning, will have a grammatical structure. Whether that grammatical structure is one that would be regarded as appropriate in writing is another matter. Reference has already been made in Chapter 2 of *English Accents and Dialects* by Arthur Hughes and Peter Trudgill, in which they list a dozen or so of the grammatical differences which distinguish standard English from non-standard dialects, and which are not usually considered appropriate in written English.

A particularly good example is afforded by the past tense of irregular verbs. Regular verbs in English have the same forms for the past tense and the past participle, thus giving,

PRESENT TENSE	PAST TENSE	PRESENT PERFECT
I love	I loved	I have loved

However, some irregular verbs have different forms for the past tense and the past participle:

PRESENT	PAST	PRESENT PERFECT
I see	I saw	I have seen
I go	I went	I have gone

As Hughes and Trudgill explain, some non-standard dialects try to bring irregular verbs into line with regular verbs, in different ways. Thus can occur:

PRESENT	PAST	PRESENT PERFECT
I see	I *seen*	I have *seen*
I *see*	I *see*	I have seen
I *come*	I *come*	I have come
I go	I *went*	I have *went*

'I seen you last night', is just as meaningful, and just as grammatical, as 'I saw you last night'. It is not, however, as acceptable in writing. Thus, those who grew up to say 'I seen you last night', must

20

learn to choose to write 'I saw you last night' if they are not to attract pejorative judgments on what they write.

At this stage of the argument, the point to be made is that the speaker who habitually says 'I seen you last night', but who wants, as a writer, to write 'I saw you last night', does not need to get from A to B in one go. There is a process known as drafting. This is the technique by which, when one is faced with the need to write, one puts down on paper roughly *what* one wants to say, without paying particular attention to the *how*. One then works on that draft until one arrives at a version in which the *how* brings out the *what* as fully as one is capable of. That is the process by which this book came to be written. In addition, a draft was given to friends for their comments, before that draft became the last, nearly final, draft. But the draft that went to friends, although called a first draft, was itself, page by page, the product of what sometimes seemed interminable re-drafting. Moreover, it is not until the proofs arrive for correction that one needs to make up one's mind finally about the *what* and the *how*.

It is a curious feature of our education system that, by the time children transfer from primary to secondary schools at 11, the idea has become deeply ingrained that writing is an activity which requires you to dash down words on paper, and then forget about them. It is a misconception that underlies the failure of so many pupils significantly to improve their ability to write during their years at secondary school. Writing has become, for them, a series of one-offs, with little or no development between.

4 'Some such rot'

Marianne Thornton, the daughter of Henry Thornton of Clapham, and the aunt of E.M. Forster, who wrote her biography, started a number of schools in Clapham in the 1860s and 1870s. 'I do not know what schools she started and financed, or partially financed, or how often she taught in them or what she taught', says E. M. Forster. But, 'After the passing of the Elementary Education Act of 1870 the scene so far clears as to reveal her coping with a new type of human being, namely the Schools Inspector'. There is an account of her meeting with one of them in a letter she wrote to her mother in March 1878, which E. M. Forster quotes:

> We've been examined all the morning by that horrid Hernaman. H[tta] was there first and when I came she whispered to me, 'I have wrung that man's neck twice over already' and so she had, convicted him of mistakes about the New Code wh. she'd studied more than he had, but it was a pity for it put him into such a cantankerous state he didn't know how to scold hard enough, said the child[n] knew nothing, nor the teachers either, and were so fidgitty — why he kept the wretches 3 hours and ½ doing nothing whatever, who wouldn't be fidgitty. But matters changed when we got to luncheon. The Rector, Erskine Clarke and Mr Sharp and I propounded the fact that most of what was taught was nonsense, specially grammar — because Hernaman had rated the child[n] for not knowing a predicate noun from an absolute or some such rot, and all joined in chorus except Hernaman, and now they are all gone.[1]

Over a hundred years ago, Marianne Thornton could say that 'most of what was taught was nonsense, specially grammar'. She had no professional qualifications as an educator, unlike, presumably, the wretched Hernaman, but saw clearly that teaching grammar, especially in the form of distinguishing 'predicate' from 'absolute' nouns, was an educational nonsense because it did not lead to improvement in the pupils' ability to use language. Yet most of the language work included in English course-books, still widely used in primary and secondary schools, is based on the supposition that, if you teach children grammatical facts about language, then their use of language will somehow improve. A lyrical statement of this belief occurs in H. B. Drake's *Foundation Exercises in English* published in 1941.

The art of teaching is largely a matter of devising exercises; grammar exercises should be considered as the scales and arpeggios, as it were, of the art of writing. Plentiful practice in the manipulation of words and constructions is the surest road to the development of a flexible and expressive prose style.

Andrew Wilkinson, in *The Foundations of Language*, summarizes 'massive research' dating from 1903 which shows that the learning of grammar has 'no beneficial effect on children's written work'.[1] One can set alongside the research results, of course, the evidence to be seen every day in the writing of pupils in school for whom the doing of grammatical exercises is having little effect on their ability to put full stops where convention demands, or to link sentences in ways that exploit the resources of the language.

This is not to assert that there should be no study of language, its sounds, its grammar, its uses, in school at all. It has already been argued that pupils in school, like all language users, possess an extensive, intuitive knowledge of language. They would not be able to use it if they did not. Making this knowledge explicit by looking closely at how language achieves its purposes can show pupils how they can extend and improve what they already do with language. But the kind of grammatical exercises incorporated in the course-books still widely used in primary and secondary schools, and still being written, published and bought, do not promote better writing. In playing about with bits and pieces of language, pupils are being prevented from finding out how to make language do what they want.

Let us take as a representative example the following exercise, from a book designed for use in primary schools, and still being bought nearly twenty years after it was first published.[3]

Singular into Plural; Plural into Singular
GROUP A

Write out these sentences, changing the words which are under-lined into the plural, and changing other words, if necessary.

1. I sent her a ripe strawberry.
2. The child had lost a tooth.
3. The lily is in the church.
4. Daily she sees the larch in the forest.

GROUP B

Write out these sentences, changing the words which are under-
lined into the singular, and changing other words if necessary.
1. We heard them singing their sad songs.
2. We watched the women; they spoke to us.
3. The daisies have shed their petals.
4. Our enemies are tearing down the flags.

What benefit are pupils supposed to derive from working through
an exercise like this? Is it designed to promote understanding of the
concept of singular and plural? Or to increase knowledge of ways
in which certain words in English indicate singularity and plu-
rality? Or to give practice in the writing of sentences? Or what?

All practice implies theory. Whatever is done in the classroom
implies learning theory. Exercises in English imply, besides, a
theory of language. Unfortunately, much of this theory is of the
folk-linguistic variety. In other words, it is on a par with the naive
assortment of beliefs about language that seem to be endemic in
our culture. Among them are beliefs about correct usage, about
the relative pleasantness of this or that dialect, and about the sort
of knowledge that should be taught about language in school.

The exercise takes for granted that the pupils understand the
concepts 'singular' and 'plural', since the words 'singular' and
'plural' are given in the title. In this assumption, the authors of the
book are probably right. The English language affords the possibility of distinguishing between singular and plural. Native
speakers of the language learn to handle this distinction as part of
their own language-learning process, although the linguistic
means by which they do so may vary according to which dialect of
English they grow up speaking. So, assuming, then, that our pupils
do understand 'singular' and 'plural', what is the exercise asking
them to do with this knowledge? To apply it to certain artificially
constructed sentences and change certain indicated words in them
from singular to plural, or vice versa. They have clearly been artificially constructed to include words like 'strawberry', 'tooth', 'larch'
and 'daisy', 'her', 'we' and 'us', which vary in their methods of
indicating the distinction between singular and plural. That they

have been artificially constructed is even more clearly demonstrated by the fact that some of them are not especially meaningful: 'I sent her a ripe strawberry.' 'I sent her some ripe strawberries,' perhaps. But *one* ripe strawberry? 'The daisies have shed their petals.' Daisies do not, as a matter of fact, shed their petals, in the plural or in the singular. 'Daily she sees the larch in the forest.' Is it an English sentence? If so, who would actually want to use it?

Again one asks the question, 'What benefit is supposed to accrue from doing exercises like this?' If the pupils already know the distinction between 'her' and 'them', between 'lily' and 'lilies', between 'they spoke to us' and 'she spoke to me', then nothing will have been gained. If they did not know that 'a ripe strawberry' becomes 'some ripe strawberries' when you have more than one, which you usually do if you have them at all, then they will presumably be told by the teacher when she goes through the exercise. But what insight will have been given into any general principles which govern the forms of nouns, pronouns and verbs as they operate in the singular or the plural?

More important, much more important, how will the doing of exercises like these increase the pupil's ability to use his own language, which is, presumably, one of the major objectives of education? The answer must surely be obvious.

Indeed, it is so obvious that the late R. J. Harris commented, when summarizing the results of his own piece of research into the effectiveness of traditional English teaching methods, 'it is surprising that conscientious teachers should continue to use its material in the classroom'.[4]

Before beginning to answer the question, and examine the insights that the answers give us, it is necessary to remind ourselves what the Bullock Report had to say about the qualifications of teachers who teach English in our secondary schools:

a third of those involved in English teaching have no discernible qualifications for the role. Of course, many of these may well be teaching English to only one or two classes, spending most of their time in some other subject. But this in itself is a significant feature and another disquieting aspect of the situation. Of the teachers engaged in English, only 37 per cent spent all their time on it. 25 per cent were teaching it more than half their time, and 38 per cent less than half.[5]

These figures were based upon the survey conducted in 1973. Six years later, they still represent fairly accurately the way in which English Departments are staffed. One other crucial consideration needs to be taken into account. It is the one raised by Principal Recommendation 15 of the Bullock Report:

> A substantial course on language in education (including reading) should be part of every primary and secondary school teacher's initial training, whatever the teacher's subject or the age of the children with whom he or she will be working.

However, in this regard, we still await what M. A. K. Halliday, in *Language and Social Man* called the 'breakthrough' in teacher training:

> There is another breakthrough still to come, in the training of teachers, who have so far been left to fend almost entirely for themselves as far as language is concerned. Perhaps we may look forward to a time when language study has some place in the professional training of all teachers, and the central place in the relevant specialist courses, especially those relating to English and to literacy ('teaching of reading').[6]

It is, then, highly likely that many English teachers will have to rely, for ideas on what kind of language work to give their pupils, on their memories of what they themselves did at school. In this, they will be abetted by the course-books that they will find in the stock cupboard, books which reproduce faithfully down the generations, as a classroom sub-culture, the kind of exercise already discussed, and described so well by James Moffett:

> Ticketing parts of speech, picking synonyms, pairing words beginning with the same sound, doctoring dummy sentence structures, underlining the simile . . . .[7]

It may well be that teachers who use these exercises not only remember them from their own school days but suppose their own English to have been improved by them. After all, they succeeded in the system, by passing exams like O level English Language. Why not, then, assume that they learnt to succeed through such activities as they themselves were engaged in? It is much more likely, however, that they were able to master the use of the writing system, as they, as all of us, learn to master the spoken language, by and for themselves. But for those of their contemporaries who did not possess this facility, the exercises were not much help. That is why they are now turning to Adult Literacy Projects in their thousands.

This belief in the use of exercises is, moreover, reinforced by the feeling that there ought to be a body of knowledge in English to be passed on to the pupils. English is unlike other academic subjects in not possessing a clearly defined teachable body of knowledge, and there is no doubt that some English teachers feel the lack of this, and try to fill the gap with definitions of Parts of Speech, of phrases and sentences, and with exercises based on them. This body of knowledge has, in the eyes of teachers, the additional merit of being examinable, as Denys Thomson pointed out in his introduction to *The Excitement of Writing*:

> There may be some subjects, such as Languages and Mathematics, in which there is an accepted and readily tested content, that are comparatively unaffected by examining. But with English there is no content, and what matters — a sensitive response to literature and life — cannot be tested by a mass-examination. So a bogus and alien content is invented and foisted on English — so alien that it would be much better if O level language tests were replaced by a foreign language. What do lend themselves to testing are knowledge of and some skill in grammar, punctuation, syntax, spelling, clause-analysis, vocabulary, precis, detecting errors . . . . As aids to reading and writing most of them are irrelevant and useless, and they squeeze out the living reading and writing that constitute any worthy course in English. How irrelevant and useless they are is brought home by a glance at some of the hundreds of African O level scripts that litter a house in which I have been staying. Scores of the writers were 95 per cent accurate on grammar, without being able to understand or write much more than pidgin English.[8]

The force of the last point is regularly demonstrated in the exercise books of native English, let alone Denys Thompson's African, pupils, where exercises in which de-contextualized statements and questions have been correctly punctuated are juxtaposed with essays in which no full stops occur.

It must be acknowledged, however, that the doing of exercises enables the teacher to set up situations in the classroom which are

27

controlled and predictable. This is not a consideration to be dismissed lightly, especially in the case of teachers 'with no discernible qualifications' for teaching English faced with the problem of keeping a third form occupied for the five periods a week which they have been given with them. The exercises rest upon a conceptual basis which teachers remember from their own school days, lead to answers which, in their own terms, can be declared right or wrong, and do not stray beyond what the teacher is familiar with. Unlike the Adult Literacy Tutor, the teacher tends to see his professional status mortgaged in his teaching methods. If the Tutor's student is not succeeding, the teaching method is changed. If the teacher's pupils fail, the blame rests with them, not the method. It is not being suggested, of course, that the situation of the teacher, with a class of thirty, is like that of the Adult Literacy Tutor with her one student. Teaching methods and class control are interrelated. When the class is under tight control, heads bend industriously over exercise books, the teacher's self-image is enhanced. The class is busily engaged in doing something likely to be approved of by senior colleagues, by parents concerned that 'standards' should be kept up, and by the pupils themselves, who have been convinced of the benefits to be derived from the discipline of work which appears to involve logical thinking. There is a transparency about the process which makes its 'value' self-evident.

These are the factors which have conspired to ensure that the kind of knowledge, and the exercises deriving from them, so aptly dismissed by Marianne Thornton over a hundred years ago as 'some such rot', still persist as a classroom sub-culture, despite the fact that they patently do little to promote the pupils' ability to handle the writing system. It is as if, long ago, the teaching of grammar became confused with the teaching of writing, and this confusion has been transmitted unthinkingly from generation to generation of teachers. As a result, too many pupils spend too much time, which could be more profitably used, doing verbal jigsaw puzzles, and being confronted by assertions like this, written on the blackboard:

Abstract
A noun that is the name for a quality is called abstract. You cannot touch an abstract noun unlike other kinds of nouns. If a person is rude we notice in turn a quality called rudeness.

How else can one explain the exercise books still to be found in which exercises designed to help pupils distinguish between 'common' and 'neuter' nouns and between 'strong' and 'weak' verbs are sandwiched between examples of writing that show little improvement in quality from the first piece to the last?

Anyone who doubts that this is representative of normal classroom practice should look at Chapter 6 of *Aspects of Secondary Education in England*, the survey published by H.M.I. in 1979. They describe, for instance, the written output of 'an able boy in the second term of his fourth year'. It is an example which could easily be replicated, with variations, from schools all over the country.

English
Written output of about 6,000 words, but including seven punctuation, thirteen comprehension, two grammar and three multiple choice exercises calling for little of the pupils' own writing.[9]

One learns to write by writing. It is only by trying to write in response to need that one can explore for oneself the two constraints, namely, what the writing system will allow, and what our own mastery of the writing system will allow us to do.

Pupils whose mastery of the writing system is less than adequate have to devote their efforts to finding ways around their weaknesses, like adults who use various strategies to conceal the fact that they cannot read. A teacher, looking at a page of writing from a twelve-year-old in which 'and' was the only conjunction used, thought to ask the pupil, 'What do you think your main weakness is?' She received the reply, 'Full stops'. Because the boy could not handle full stops, he resorted to the device of joining all his sentences with 'and'. In consequence, his writing was seen as immature, even babyish. If someone had earlier found a way of teaching him how to use full stops, he would, in Mina Shaughnessy's splendid phrase, have been 'released' into the writing system, which he might have learned to handle with a confidence approaching that with which, no doubt, he handled speech.

5 Writing in school

After three years of schooling at Barbiana I took, in June, my exams for the intermediate diploma as a private-school candidate. The composition topic was: 'The Railway Waggons Speak'. (*Letter to a Teacher* by the School of Barbiana[1])

Composition for Homework: A Day in the Life of a Parking Meter

i

Writing is doing, a linguistic activity normally engaged in by an individual who is responding to a demand, and who is literate enough to switch into the written mode to make that response. In adult life, the demand may arise from one's job, from one's role as taxpayer, friend, father or mother, complainant, enquirer, or from a desire to write as poet, novelist or playwright. In every case, there will be a function for the writing to perform, and an audience to whom it is to be addressed. From function and audience can be derived ideas of what will constitute appropriate form and style; what we have called 'mastery of the writing system' implies the ability to make informed judgments on appropriacy.

How does the situation of the writer so described compare with the situation of the pupil in school? We will take as an example the situation of pupils transferring at 11 + from primary to secondary school. They are not in the situation of the child in Roger McGough's poem 'Snipers' who 'started school and became an infant' at the age of 5, but the line is a splendid reminder that children of school age live in two worlds, the world of school and, one is tempted to say, the 'real' world outside.

Pupils entering secondary school from primary school will encounter a substantial difference at once. Instead of having one teacher for most of the time, as they will have been used to in each year of primary school, they will find their week in secondary school divided up between more than ten teachers, of English, of French, of History, of Geography, of Maths, of Science, of P.E., of R.E., of Art, of the various Craft subjects. Many of these will be asking for writing, perhaps in the first week. What will the pupils, when faced with these demands, be able to assume?

Will they be able to assume that the nature and purpose of the writing which is being demanded will be clearly defined? That there will be a consistency about the way in which the writing is received and treated by the different teachers? That guidance will be offered as to how the writing falls short of what is expected? That effectively relevant help will be given to help pupils overcome deficiencies in their grasp of the writing system?

The answers which may be given to any or all of the questions will depend on the views of the writing process held by the individual teachers with whom pupils will come into contact. It is, five years after the publication of the Bullock Report, unlikely that the school will have an effective language policy that includes an overall view of, and policy towards, the writing demands made on pupils. The Secondary Survey confirms this.[2] There may be departmental policies governing aspects of language and learning in particular subjects, but even within departments, including English departments, there can be no guarantee that a consistent treatment of writing will obtain. This will continue to be the case while the teacher's view of writing derives from the kind of intellectual framework described in Chapter 4.

This is, as we have seen, an oversimplified view, being little more than the belief that writing is writing, which some pupils are good at and others not. There are those specialist teachers in secondary schools who believe that writing, somehow, exists independently of their subject, and that all they have to do is to inject their subject content into a pre-existing ability to write. Of course, before a pupil can begin to write anything at all about, say, William the Conqueror, there must be some ability to represent words on paper in a form that carries meaning to the reader. But to suppose that there is little or no relationship between *what* one might want to write about William the Conqueror and *how* one might want to write it at two o'clock on a Monday afternoon in a school in Warrington is naive.

What, for a start, is the point of writing about William the Conqueror at two o'clock on a Monday afternoon in a school in Warrington, or anywhere else? Has the teacher explained it to himself, let alone the pupils? If he has explained it to the pupils, has that explanation been sufficiently detailed to leave the pupils in no doubt as to why they are writing, to whom, and in what form? How far, in other words, has the teacher put his pupils in a position to write? What opportunities have they had, or will they have, to discuss what they want to write with the teacher, or with each other? What advice have they had about drafting? What will happen to the writing that has been done by 2.45, when the bell goes, and the class has to move to a Geography lesson and perhaps write about Australia?

Such questions might be put to all subject-teachers who ask their pupils to write. Their answers, taken together, would give a clear indication of how much sense pupils entering secondary school might be expected to make of the demands made on their writing, to which they might then begin to produce an organized response.

But having responded, perhaps ten times in a week in different subjects, what then? What we have called the naive view of writing held by some teachers could have very damaging consequences for the pupils. If teachers believe that the *how* of writing is none of their business, that their business is simply to teach History, or Geography, or whatever, then those pupils who still need help in mastering the writing system may be in difficulty, unless they can be certain of obtaining the help they need from other sources. The difficulty is greatest for those pupils who do not qualify for 'remedial' help but whose English teachers believe in a combination of 'exercises' and self-help. They may go through secondary school without ever getting the help they need, help that is both relevant to their needs and effective.

The 'self-help' school of thought is symbolized by the injunction 'watch your spelling' or 'watch your punctuation' written at the end of a piece of written work. It is sometimes possible to see this legend written after every piece of work in an exercise book, with no discernible improvement between the first and last pieces. It is probable that, if pupils could 'watch their spelling' they would. Apart from directing attention to the odd slip that all of us make from time to time, the inscription does no more than signal the message that the teacher regards spelling as in some way important. But not important enough to do something effective about it.

Injunctions to self-help are not enough. A diet of 'exercises' is no substitute for positive, relevant and effective help. Unless such help is forthcoming, the outlook for some pupils will be gloomy; they may well enter their fifth and, for some, last year at school showing little improvement over what they could do at 11. Their plight is eloquently expressed in this extract from a letter, one of hundreds received by the BBC from pupils in school requesting help from the Adult Literacy Project.

I have troble in spelling and reading and I wonder if you could help me. I am 14 years old and soon I will be getting a job but I would not be able to get a good job because of the forms to pass for an engineer so I wonder if you could get someone to help me.

ii

The vet said he had an increbil desicds and that he was going to die.   (First version)

The vet said he only had 6 hours to live.   (Final version)

The girl was writing an essay on 'Pets', telling a story that may well have been autobiographical. At the teacher's request, she, like all the other members of the class, wrote out a version in rough before writing out the version that was to be handed in. The class was told that the work could be finished for homework, but this young lady sensibly made sure that she had finished by the end of the lesson. What the pupils were engaged in was not drafting in the sense in which it was discussed in Chapter 3, although the two versions quoted at the top of the page appear to represent a genuine piece of drafting. The girl had tried her hand at writing what she wanted to mean, but had decided, on reflection, that 'increbil desicds' probably did not 'look right'. She, therefore, intelligently altered it, in the process revealing that she understood the nature of drafting.

This kind of intuitive understanding is, however, all too rarely allowed to develop. When pupils enter secondary school, they are for the most part already convinced that writing entails putting on paper what you might want to say, and leaving it at that — unless you have been told to do a version in rough first. It is then not unknown for the final version to contain more infelicities than the rough version, since it has been written out more quickly. In such manner are pupils denied the opportunity to explore how the process of writing works for them, and how they may gain control over it.

Materials developed by the Learning Materials Service of the Inner London Education Authority suggest a way in which pupils in their first term in secondary schools might, in contrast, be given this opportunity.[3] The question was asked, 'What kind of writing project might introduce first-form pupils to the concepts of context and audience, and entail a process of drafting in order to produce an acceptable final version?' The first idea to be tried in schools was the production of a pamphlet, intended for the pupils in the top forms of those primary schools which the first-formers had left the previous July. Thus a context was created, within which the purpose of the writing could be made clear. After two months in their new school, the youngsters knew the kind of information and guidance they would have welcomed in their first weeks. They were, in fact, being put in the position of experts passing on the benefit of their experience to those who were coming after. The audience was clearly defined, and the fact that the pamphlet was to be sent to other schools meant that every effort had to be made with the presentation.

This is how the advisory teacher in charge of the project, Martin Chilcott, described the various stages in an early draft:

Suggestions are made to the pupils about how they can help one another to plan their writing, and to improve it, before actually sending it off. The motivation of getting a response to their writing provides incentive to take the time and care to redraft and achieve higher standards in what they select to write about, how they express it, and the accuracy of spelling, punctuation and general presentation.

The text of the booklets is addressed to the children but the project relies on the teachers directing, timing and guiding the pupils in their various individual and group activities. The children's initial work falls into the following broad stages:

Planning how to find someone to write to

The class assess their readers or 'audience' through discussion and note taking

⇩

In groups the children discuss what they are going to write about and how they are going to write it. They are encouraged to order their ideas through note making

⇩

Each child writes a first draft

⇩

Each child checks through a sample first draft and then discusses with the class what alterations they would make to it.

⇩

More sample drafts to edit are included for further class or group editing if required

⇩

In groups the children collaborate to check on each other's drafts, and each child makes his/her second draft.

⇩

Each child reads about proof reading, and in groups the children practise using proof marks on the samples provided.

⇩

More sample drafts to proof read are included for further group or individual work if required.

⇩

In groups the children proof mark each other's work and each child writes their final copy.

⇩

The writing is sent to the audience

This project for 11 – 14 year olds should take from 3 – 8 weeks to complete depending on how many lessons are devoted to it.

It would appear from the initial trial in a number of schools that a project like this does succeed in bringing pupils to a greater understanding of the writing process, and of their involvement in their own writing. They learn that writing is something that has to be worked at if they are to achieve a satisfactory end product. They also learn that coming to this satisfactory end product requires genuine collaboration between themselves and their teacher, with the teacher offering advice and help that are seen to be relevant and effective. The lessons thus learnt can be regularly reinforced by getting pupils to write for an audience outside the classroom. Occasions can be found or created: form, year or school newspapers or anthologies; projects in the form of exhibitions which demand certain kinds of writing; competitions at school, local or national level.

It will be noticed that proof-reading is introduced as part of the process, with the most commonly used proof-reading symbols being taught. Pupils are encouraged to proof-read their own, and each other's, work, before it is seen by the teacher. The three most useful symbols are:

    $\land$ meaning 'insert what is written in the margin'.

    $\mathcal{G}$ meaning 'delete what is crossed out'.

    np meaning 'begin new paragraph'.

Others can be taught as appropriate.[4]

Collaborative writing* has another, massive, advantage. It genuinely enables the pupils to invest their language in the fulfilment of the task that they have been asked to undertake, in contrast to the traditional exercises plus essay approach, which effectively denies the pupils access to what operational knowledge of language they have.

It is a paradox that it should be thought necessary to teach grammar in order that pupils should learn to write, when, as M. A. K. Halliday points out, 'spoken language is on the whole more complex than written language in its grammar . . . .'

At first sight this seems surprising, since we are accustomed to thinking of written language as having the more complex syntax of the two. But it is not really surprising when one takes into account the nature of the two media. Writing is a deliberate and, even with modern technology, a relatively slow process; the text is created as an object, and is perceived by the reader as an object — it exists. Spoken text does not exist; it happens. The text is created and is perceived by the listener, as a process. Its

*(Working in groups — see Appendix, p. 70)

reference points are constantly shifting: the speaker keeps on going, and the listener cannot pause and hold up the text for contemplation — he is carried along with it, tracking the process as it happens. The reader, of course, also has to keep moving; but in this case it is he and not the writer who determines the pace. So, while speech and writing can both be very complex, the complexities tend to be of different kinds. The complexity of speech is choreographic — an intricacy of movement. That of writing is crystalline — a denseness of matter. In linguistic terms, spoken language is characterized by complex sentence structures with low lexical density (more clauses, but fewer high content words per clause); written language by simple sentence structures with high lexical density (more high content words per clause, but fewer clauses). We could express this even more briefly, though at the cost of distorting it somewhat, by saying that speech has complex sentences with simple words, while writing has complex words in simple sentences.[5]

Writing projects which require collaboration and discussion at every stage, as well as formal outcomes in both spoken and written language, are especially valuable. A good example is the planning of an advertising campaign for an invented product which would require the designing of advertisements to appear in magazines and colour supplements, to be screened on television and to be broadcast on commercial radio. Another is a project involving research into, and dramatization of, a historical incident, preferably one with local connections.[6] The kind of assignment being developed for Communication Studies, in which data have to be collected, evaluated and discussed before various written responses have to be made is another useful vehicle, while numerous suggestions may be found in *Language and Use* and *Using Language in Use*.[7]

Responsibility for the development of pupils' writing ability rests mainly, though not exclusively, with the English department. Not exclusively, for every teacher who asks for writing from pupils has a responsibility towards the development of indivdual writing abilities. In one of its best known recommendations in *A language for life* the Bullock Committee insisted that 'every secondary school should develop a policy for language across the curriculum. The responsibility for this policy should be embodied in the organizational structure of the school.'[8] Such a policy must clearly have something to say about writing, about what is asked for, about the way in which it should be dealt with by the teacher, and about the provision of effective help for those who need it. H.M.I.'s Secondary Survey makes it clear that this recommendation has been little implemented. Nevertheless, there should be a policy which ensures that no pupil, in any subject, should be asked to write unless the purpose of the writing has been clearly explained and unless there is adequate time for the pupils to produce an acceptable draft.

The policy should, by laying down guidelines for assessment and marking, ensure that in any given school the pupils' writing will be received and dealt with in much the same way by all their teachers. The fact that the term 'marking' is still in common use is very significant. Head teachers and parents sometimes complain that the pupils' work has not been 'marked', as if the act of marking a pupil's work has, of itself, any educational significance. The fact is that teachers, English teachers in particular, waste a great deal of their time 'marking' work in the traditional way, as part of the teacher's role. They waste it, because the marking is not followed by learning, witness exercise books which show no improvement from beginning to end, despite the assiduous 'marking' of spelling and punctuation mistakes, together with such marginal injunctions as 'Watch your spelling' or 'Not enough full stops'. (One of my colleagues once saw an exercise book in which 'Do not use ampersands' had been written at the bottom of every essay, including the one which came at the end of the book.)

It would be a useful step forward to abandon the term *marking* in favour of *assessment*, for what the pupil requires, above all, is an assessment of how close his work has come to the teacher's expectations when the task was set.

In Chapter 3, a distinction was drawn, following Mina Shaughnessy, between the *how* and the *what*. In other words, two questions are being asked about a piece of writing. How is the writer using the writing system? What is the meaning he is trying to convey? This distinction makes a useful basis for assessment. As adopted by some English departments, it takes the form of a two-symbol five-point system, $A - E$ for the *what*, $1 - 5$ for the *how*. Thus, a pupil who has come close to fulfilling expectations as to the *what* may be given A, but since it has been idiosyncratically spelt and contains few full stops it merits only 5 for the *how*. It therefore receives A5. On the other hand, a pupil who has missed the point of the activity but shows mastery of the writing system might receive E1. In both cases, of course, it will be incumbent upon the teacher to offer relevant advice and make the necessary help available.

Teachers, when 'marking', seem to look only for what is *wrong*, sometimes relentlessly, no matter how slight the deviation from what is thought to be right. Assessment, on the other hand looks for evidence of what is right, or nearly right. This distinction was beautifully illustrated by Antony Hopkins, talking about Sir Michael Tippett in a programme broadcast on New Year's Day, 1980. When, as a pupil, said Mr Hopkins, he took his attempts at musical composition to Sir Michael, he was never told, 'That's wrong'. The comment would be rather, 'You've got a bit of a problem there'. The difference is crucial for the pupil, in particular for his attitude to his own achievement. There is nothing so demoralizing as having attention drawn, week after week, to what you have got wrong, especially if you are getting no help in putting it right. It is not uncommon to see the comment, 'Watch your spelling', on a piece of writing which has only one spelling mistake in it, the presence of four hundred correctly spelt words going quite unremarked.

A piece of writing produced by a pupil should be regarded as evidence of what the he can do at the time it is produced. The job of the teacher is, on the basis of that evidence, to try to see that the next piece of writing is better. The assessment needs to be done with sensitivity and discrimination, with teachers being ready to trust their own judgment.

According to the status of the writing, and where it comes in the programme of work, teachers should know what emphasis to place on the various features of the pupils' attempts to make meaning in writing. How far has the pupil succeeded in conveying his/her meaning? Is it the meaning the teacher was looking for? Is it appropriately expressed? If not, what is getting in the way?

This suggests that the teacher should have in mind a hierarchy of errors, with the most serious those that impede the reader's access to the meaning intended by the writer and the least serious those that may merely irritate the reader, e.g. alright for all right. Traditional marking insists that equal attention be drawn to every error, no matter how serious or how trivial. Thus, even if pupils know how, or are being helped, to overcome their weaknesses, they have no notion of where to start. Marking merely draws attention to what is seen by the teacher as being wrong. One can only suppose that this is for the benefit of the teachers themselves, or their Heads, or the parents of the pupils. Its purpose is not for the benefit of the pupils, since normally nothing happens as a result. The same errors are reproduced week after week, year after year.

When, in contrast, pupils understand that what their teachers are doing when they draw attention to features of their writing is offering help in overcoming problems, a genuine learning partnership can be set up.

Pupils will know that their work will be judged sympathetically, that its merits will be recognized, that its shortcomings will be described, and that effective help will be forthcoming to enable them to remedy the shortcomings. Nothing succeeds like success, and the first step to success is the recognition that one is making progress. The Adult Literacy Tutor is taught to teach for success, to ensure, as far as possible, that the student can do something at the end of the session that he or she could not do at the beginning, and to recognize the achievement.

It is attitudes like these, on the part of both teacher and taught, that make for educational success, attitudes like these which might ensure that pupils do not leave secondary school writing little better than they did when they entered the school five years previously.

6   Relevant and effective help

Much has already been said about the importance of offering to pupils help that is both relevant and effective — relevant to their own educational needs, and effective in that it actually promotes learning. In this chapter, ways of doing this are discussed, beginning with spelling and punctuation, the 'terrible twins' as they are sometimes called. Then, since it has been argued that a naive concern with Parts of Speech wastes valuable time in which real development of writing ability might be taking place, their role in the mythology of English teaching is considered. Finally, there is a note on dialect, and its supposed interference with the ability to learn to write.

Spelling

13 september   <u>Spellings</u>

rouse ✓   ummedaghtely ✗   circle ✓
happily ✓   woendering ✗   actuly ✗
crackel ✗   opportunaty ✗   erat' crawl ✓
querquat ✗   preparation ✓   scerday ✗
conceal ✓   excoice ✗

Do your homework thoroughly   b/10

41

This is the second piece of work in the exercise book of a first-former in a secondary school. There is nothing to suggest why this collection of words was set for homework rather than any other. Under the next exercise has been written 'see me', and under the next-but-one 'more care needed'. As the year proceeds, and the boy's spelling shows no signs of improving, the teacher's comments become increasingly exasperated. 'Care needed with spelling . . . much more care needed . . . MUCH more care needed'. There is, however, no evidence, at least in the exercise book, that the teacher's exasperation has driven her to try to show the boy *how* to take more care.

This is the traditional way of approaching spelling: draw attention to the mistake, urge the pupil (with or without the injunction to write it out three, five or ten times) to learn the correct spelling, and leave it at that. Rarely are pupils shown how they might go about it successfully. Once again, it is the Adult Literacy Tutors who have pointed the way.

Catherine Moorhouse, in *Helping Adults to Spell*, sums up their philosophy:

> It is doubtful whether you can *teach* someone to spell; but certain that you can show someone *how to learn* to spell. There is no one system which can guarantee to improve a person's spelling, simply because each of us has a unique set of learning styles, and we tend to use different spelling strategies depending upon the word in question. The next section of this book will describe and illustrate a variety of techniques you can try with your student, and he can try for himself. Some of them he may not like, or you may not like, in which case ignore them. It doesn't really matter *how* he learns to spell as long as he is eventually able to *recognize* (the sounds), *recall* (the letters), and *reproduce in writing* the words he wants to use. If he becomes a really 'good' speller, he will eventually do this automatically. The most important rule about 'teaching' spelling is: DON'T ASK A STUDENT TO LEARN A WORD WITHOUT SHOWING HIM A WAY OF DOING SO.[1]

Mike Torbe adopts a similar approach in *Teaching Spelling*, a title which places responsibility with the teacher, whose job 'is not to correct mistakes the pupil has already made, but to help him not to make that mistake next time.'[2]

The starting point must always be with the spelling offered by the pupil. Most of them spell consistently, if not orthographically. This means that they have memorized a sequence of letters that for them corresponds with the sound of the word. For the most part (as with the examples at the head of this section) there is little difficulty in deciphering the word, because a correspondence between sound and symbol that conveys an adequate suggesion of the intended word has been achieved.

Thus in the exercise above we have

'crackel'	for	'crackle'
'quater'	for	'quarter'
'immedaghtly'	for	'immediately'
'woundering'	for	'wondering'
'opportunaty'	for	'opportunity'
'exosice'	for	(presumably) 'exercise'
'actuly'	for	'actually'
and 'scercly'	for	'scarcely'

If one is to offer effective help to the boy when asking him to relearn the way in which he spells these words, the first essential is to see where the spelling that has been offered deviates from the spelling that is expected, and, if possible, why. Then an appropriate learning strategy may be devised.

The simplest kind is a display designed to draw attention to similarities between the visual patterns of words which the pupil gets right and the target word. If a pattern can be found which enforces the learner's attention to what is causing the difficulty, so much the better.[3]

'Crackel' is easy. On the analogy of 'barrel', 'el' is a permissible ending, although not in 'crackle'. (Perhaps 'cracker-barrel is causing interference!) A display like

crack
crackle_
tackle_

may be enough to promote the desired learning. If not, another strategy will be needed. What works with one pupil may not work with another, as Catherine Moorhouse points out.

Why 'quater' for 'quarter'? On the analogy of 'water'? If so, this display suggest itself:

wart

quart

quarter

In 'immedaghtely' the intrusion of 'gh' is difficult to explain. It is possible that the boy pronounces 'immediate', as do many people, with a sound in the middle like the initial sound of 'judge', and that this has caused uncertainty about the spelling. Perhaps this would help:

media

immediate

immediately

In 'woundering' it is not clear in the text whether the 'u' has been crossed out. This suggests a confusion caused by words like 'under' and 'wound', leading to uncertainty in 'wonder'. Since we have 'won', this might help:

won

wonder

wondering

'Opportunaty', which may have been influenced by a word like 'fortunately', differs in respect of only one letter from the approved spelling. To suggest the '-ity' ending, a display like

city

felicity

opportunity

might be helpful.

It is tempting to suggest that the boy's spelling of 'exercise' has been subject to interference from 'exorcise', but this is hardly likely. His offering, 'exosice', reveals two separate uncertainties. The first is about the appropriate way in which to render the unstressed vowel sound in the middle of the word, while the second may have been brought on by well-meaning attempts to get him to discriminate between the use of 'c' and 's' in a pair like license/licence. Attention might be drawn by means of a display like

He was exercising his dog

He exercised his dog

The exercise did him good

He exerted himself

44

For 'actuly', the display

    actu<u>al</u>

    actu<u>ally</u>

    factu<u>ally</u>

might do.
While for 'scercly' the pairing of

    sc<u>arce</u>

    sc<u>arce</u>ly

might do the trick.

It is not being suggested that English teachers should devise an appropriate learning strategy for every word misspelt by every pupil they take for English. That would be an intolerable burden, and unnecessary. For one thing, there is a body of English words that, judging by the frequency with which they are misspelt, seems to present special difficulties. Lists of them can be found in many school books. A better, because more relevant, way of determining which they are is to arrange with all the teachers who ask for writing from, say, the first year group in a school to collect the misspellings which occur in the writing in the course of two weeks. Strategies can then be worked out for the most common. If they are sorted into categories, individual members of the English Department may take a category each, in this way building up a departmental repertoire of strategies in the form of cards for particular words, or groups of words, that contain a variety of learning strategies.

There will be, in all probability, four main categories of mistake: words which are confused because they sound alike and have minimal discrimination in the writing system (e.g. their/there; two/too/to); words in which there is uncertainty about 'double letters', (e.g. necessary, harass, embarrass, accommodation); words in which there is 'interference' from speech (e.g. peculiar spelt as 'perculiar'); and the so-called 'phonic mismatches', in which a correspondence has been made between sound and symbol which is allowable in some words, although not in the word in question, as is the example already quoted, 'inshoerance' for insurance. The number of books to which teachers can turn for helpful suggestions is continually growing.[4]

If such a project were to be undertaken in the first term in secondary school, it is likely that a significant improvement in the general level of spelling would result, although individual, even idiosyncratic, problems would remain. These would require individual treatment, for which opportunity would need to be made.

Positive use needs to be made, at all times, of a neglected resource, the pupils themselves. They need to be let in on the act, and encouraged to take responsibility for their own learning as part of a genuine collaboration between pupil and teacher. They need to be shown how to develop what Catherine Moorhouse in her chapter, Working on Writing, in the *BBC Writing and Spelling Handbook*,[4] calls 'a thinking attitude to spelling'.

But pupils cannot develop 'a thinking attitude to spelling' unless their teachers have done so first. Their 'thinking attitude' must encompass the ability both to diagnose the cause of a misspelling and to prescribe a remedy. It should enable the teacher to see a 'mistake' as evidence of knowledge, for, as John Keen insists in *Teaching English: a linguistic perspective*, 'one cannot make a mistake in something unless one can do it fairly well to begin with. I can make a mistake in speaking French because I can speak a little French. I cannot make a mistake in speaking Hindi because I can speak no Hindi at all.'[5]

Before a 'mistake' can be seen as evidence of knowledge, teachers must be able to place it in the system to which it relates. They must thus possess knowledge of that system, that is, a genuinely linguistic understanding, rather than a mythological view, of the English spelling system. There are several sources to which they can refer.

The most accessible is the chapter called 'The English Writing System', in the Teachers' manual to *Breakthrough to Literacy*.[6] This draws upon K. H. Albrow's *The English Writing System* (number 2 of the second series of papers produced by the Schools Council Programme in Linguistics and English Teaching),[7] in which the author offers a description of English spelling which goes a long way towards explaining what he calls 'the apparent complexities of the English writing system'. He begins by asking 'What one should and should not expect of any writing system', and asserts firmly, 'One thing that should not be expected of a writing system is that it should write down the sounds of the language, in anything near to a literal sense of the phrase "write down the sounds".'

When we understand what the writing system is trying to do, we can understand better how it tries to do it. We can then make more sense of its patterns, the patterns that it must have if it is to work at all. For too long the English spelling system has been regarded as more difficult than it actually is, treated, as M.A.K. Halliday says, 'as an enemy, as a monster to be placated; and we see the child who is just becoming literate as an innocent victim of its arbitrary tyranny'.[8] While teachers continue to communicate this belief to their pupils, they will encourage them to regard misspelling as an act of fate which they can do little to remedy.

The following passage was written by a boy during his English exam at the end of his fourth year in secondary school.

Violence of Today

Violence today is widespread among young people, because they are bored and they are looking for something to do. They blame society for this, so they hit back and they want to rebel against the system.

There are many places where violence appears, ranging from smashed windows to crime. In estates you usually find violent scenes. Generally this is usually about their favourite football teams or it's just foul language. The football team is the favourite for violence. The supporter loyal to his team will fight for his club, just for the colours the bloke on the other side's wearing.

Crime is linked to violent scenes. Most crime today is done by the young people, and this crime is anything but petty theft. The ages where most of these crimes arise are between the ages of 13 to 17 years old. These range from Taking and Driving Away, Grievous Bodily Harm, Carrying an Offensive Weapon, Hitting an Officer, Drunken Driving and Trespassing. The ones that appear most frequently are T.D.A. and G.B.H. You find that it is not just one kid on his own, but a couple just out for a laugh. Taking and Driving Away is very serious, because the person who is driving might not or will not have any insurance, so if he runs anyone over or if he causes an accident he is not covered, so whoever he hits does not get a penny compensation. And the person who has lost their husband or their wife may have two to three kids to look after. I think that they should find out where most of these kids originate from, and then start, you could say, to deprogramme them. Because something somewhere is rough, the kids have no thought for anyone else. They just live from day to day. So if they get into that system, what are they going to be like when they grow up? On the dole. As long as they've got money for cigarettes and beer they're all right. Then comes the problem of the wife or the girlfriend.

The problem is how to deprogramme an outcast of society. One way I think is to put them in a surrounding that they want to be part of, somewhere where they won't have to be tough to survive, like in the ghettos. They can just be themselves, somewhere where they will be taught some consideration not just to look after themselves but others as well. To be taught some priorities.

Readers might, at this point, care to assess the essay for themselves. What evidence does it provide of the boy's mastery of the writing system?

That, however, was not as it was written. The original was spelt like this. Is not the boy entitled to spell better than this after ten years in school? And if he could spell better, how much more use could he make of the writing system?

Violence of Today

Violence today is widespread amounge younge people, because they are bored and they are looking for something to do. They blame society for this so they hit back and they wont to rebale at the sistem.

There are many places were violence apears, ranging from smashed windows to crime. In astates you usually fined violent sens, grafely this is usually about there faverat football teams or it's just foull language.

The football team is the faverat for violence, the supporter loyal to his team will fight for his club just for the collers the block on the other sides wearing.

Crime is linked to violent sens. Most crime today is done today by the younge people and this crime is aneything but petty theft. The ages were most of these crime arrise at are bettween the age of 13 to 17 year old's. These range from Tacken and driving away, greveus bodaly harm, Careing a ofensive wepun, Hiting an Ofiser, Drunken Driving and Trespasing.

The ones that apper most frequent are T.D.A. and G.B.H. you find that it not just one kid on his owen but a cuppel just out for a laf. Tacking and Driving away is very sereac becuse the pearson who is driving mite not or will not have any inshoerance, so if he run's any one over or if he causes a accedent he is not coverered so who ever he hits dose not get a peney compansation. And the person who has lost their husband or taeir wife, may have two to three kids to look after.

I think that they should find out were most of these kids erigenat from and then start you could say to deprogram them because something some were is rogh the kids have no thought for anyone else they just live from day today, so if they get into that sestem wot are they going to be lick when they grow up, on the dowell as long as thave got money for cigerate and bear there allright.

Then comes the problem of the wife or the girlfriend. The problem is how to deprogram a outcast of sociaty, one way I think is to put them in a ceronding that they wont to be part of somewere were they wont have to be tough to survive lick in the getos. They just be themselves, somewere were they will be taught some concideration not just to look after themselves but others as well. To be tought some priorateas.

Punctuation

It is a convention of written English that 'sentences' should begin with a capital letter and end with a full stop. Some pupils acquire the habit, some do not. At least, that appears to be the case, since many fifth-formers continue to mark the ends of sentences with commas, despite having their attention drawn regularly to the preference of the writing system for full stops.

'More full stops, please.'

'Where are the full stops?'

There seem to be three ways in which, either singly, or in combination, the problem is tackled in school. They are, (1) through definitions of 'the sentence'; (2) through exercises of the 'Add full stops and capital letters to the following passage' type, the passage being a chunk of somebody else's writing from which the stops and capitals have been omitted; and (3) through misleading suggestions on how to use pauses in speech as a guide to punctuation.

There are two drawbacks to approaching the full stop through definition of the sentence. One is the difficulty of arriving at an acceptable definition, and the other is that any such definitions work, if they work at all, at a high level of abstraction. If the pupil can understand them, it is unlikely that he is having difficulties with full stops. Definitions of this type include, 'A sentence is a complete thought', or 'A sentence is a unit of language which must make complete sense', or 'A sentence is a group or combination of words capable of expressing a judgement', or 'In a sentence something must be said about something'. Frank Palmer deals with the inequacy of such definitions in *Grammar*.

> How do we know what a complete thought is? Is 'cabbage' or 'man' a complete thought? If not, why not? And is 'If it rains I shan't come' one thought, or two joined together? It would seem quite impossible to provide any definition along these lines. Equally it is impossible to provide a logical definition for the sentence. One such would be that it contains a subject and predicate — that on the one hand it indicates something that we are talking about, and on the other it says something about it. For instance, in 'John is coming' we are talking about John, the subject, and also saying that he is coming, the predicate. The difficulty here is that if this definition is to be of any use we must be able to identify what we are talking about, and very often we talk about several things at once. For instance, in the sentence, 'John gave the book to Mary' we are clearly talking about John, the book, and Mary and all three might be the subject.[9]

Clearly, the approach to the full stop through definitions of the sentence is not likely to prove helpful.

In any case, it is not the inability of pupils to write in sentences that is in question, contrary to what is sometimes said, despite the clear evidence on the page of words organized in complete grammatical structures. What is in question is their seeming inability to mark the beginnings and ends of their sentences in the appropriate way. In other words, it is not so much a problem of language structure as a problem of lay-out. When seen in those terms, it becomes apparent why the traditional approaches do not succeed: they do not tackle the real problem.

David Crystal, in *Child Language, Learning and Linguistics*, suggests that

> punctuation (and associated features such as spacing and layout) becomes less of a problem if it can be related systematically to the intonation system of the language, which is the main means the child has previously had of *delimiting and linking grammatical structures*. (my italics)[10]

This approach, besides attacking the real problem, has the great merit of enabling pupils to make use of what they already know about language in the spoken form in order to improve their mastery of the written form.

Those who can speak a language understand the use that language makes of intonation to convey meaning. Thus, competent speakers of English know, for example, that what is represented in writing as

John is coming,

and looks like a statement, can be uttered as question by the use of an intonation pattern in which the voice rises at the end of 'coming'. Likewise, competent speakers of English know that utterances can be given different meanings by stressing different words, or parts of words. Thus, in the sentence,

She made him work,

the following meanings can be conveyed by different placing of the stress:

SHE made him work	—	It was 'she' rather than anyone else who made him work.
She MADE him work	—	She compelled him; she didn't ask, or persuade, him.
She made HIM work	—	She made 'him' work, if nobody else.
She made him WORK	—	An exclamation of surprise that she could have made him work.

One successful programme of work designed to lead up to full stops began with the soccer results as read on the radio on Saturday evenings during the winter. It is usually possible to predict, from the way in which the announcer intones the name of the home team, whether the result is a home win, an away win, or a draw. By recording the results, preparing a tape which consists only of the home teams, playing it to a class, and asking them to guess the result, attention can be focused on the intonation pattern.

The next stage of this 'attack' upon full stops consisted of a series of sentences like 'John is coming' and 'she made him work', designed to explore how different meanings can be given by emphasizing and stressing this word or that, and how the same words can be made to ask a question, make a statement or issue a command by altering the intonation pattern. This kind of work, best done in pairs or small groups, is, of course, oral. At some point, the switch must be made to written. The first step is for pupils to make up, and write down, their own short sentences for presentation to their partners. Capital letters and full stops (or question marks) must be insisted upon — and pupils are sometimes keener on insisting than their teachers! Thus, the visual representation of short sentences, which take up no more than one line, will become familiar.

The need, after this, is to help the pupil to invest the familiarity they have acquired in a task which requires the writing of short sentences in a context which gives some validity to the task. A script for a radio play which has five or six characters making short contributions is an obvious example, set out like this:

Tom:	Who's going on the trip?
Jane:	I am.
Tom:	I'll put you down, then.
Pat:	How much will it cost?
Jane:	About five pounds, I think.
John:	No, it's only four-fifty.
George:	I can't go, I'm afraid.
Tom:	What about you, Mary?
Mary:	Yes, I'd like to go.

Scripts for short radio plays should be written in small groups, rehearsed and performed. The writing task will thus be seen by pupils to perform a function, and the process of writing, rehearsing and reading the play will enforce attention to the lay-out of sentences. Development of the scene may be used to encourage longer sentences.

At the same time, attention should be focused on the use made of full stops in the writing of others. This may be done either through *group* discussion of missing punctuation in a passage (an overhead projector is very valuable for this, as it is for group drafting) or by adapting a passage for a form of Cloze procedure. If, say, the last word, or words, of every sentence have been omitted, discussion can centre on possible alternatives. Detailed discussion of sentence structure may be initiated through Shannon's Game, as suggested in Unit D2 of *Language in Use*, with attention concentrated on sentence-endings.[11]

Order in sentences
This unit is concerned with the basic fact that language works because much of what we say is predictable.

The aim is to explore the ways in which we make predictions from what we have heard already about what is to come next.

1. This session shows how the occurrence of words in sentences can be predicted with different degrees of probability. This is done by playing the guessing game known as Shannon's Game. Put on the board a number of dashes equal in number to the number of words in a sentence known only to the teacher, such as 'I like sugar in my tea', 'There will be bright periods with occasional showers' or 'The prince turned into a frog'. The class should be asked to guess each word in turn, with the teacher recording the number of guesses required. When this number reaches fifteen for any word, the teacher should supply the word and move to the next.

2. In this session the exploration proceeds by focusing upon
    (a) the different probabilities of 'form' words and 'content' words
    (b) how the occurrence of some words means that certain other words are likely to follow
    (c) how some features, like a plural subject, a past tense, or a comparative adjective, will immediately determine others.

    For (a) use Shannon's Game with sentences in which either the 'content' words or the 'form' words have been omitted, such as 'There will be — — with — —' or '— — — bright periods — occasional showers'.

    For (b) use sentences like 'I posted the letter in the pillar-box on the corner.' The work on (a) and (b) will provide sufficient examples of (c) for the needs of the discussion.

What is being suggested, then, is an approach to the full stop in two stages:

(1) an exploration of the intonation patterns of English, with the object of enabling pupils to make explicit to themselves the knowledge that enables them to use the intonation system to convey meaning through language organized in structures;

(2) the investment of this new, explicit, awareness in writing tasks that enforce attention, in the first instance, to the layout of short sentences, and, subsequently, to longer sentences.

The mistake is often made of mounting a full-scale attack on punctuation, which includes, besides the full stop, half a dozen uses of the comma, the semi-colon and the colon. But it is the use of the full stop that needs attention first. Once understanding of how to mark off sentences has been achieved, attention can then be switched to ways in which punctuation is used within sentences to indicate meaning by marking off groups of words.

Parts of Speech and the teaching of grammar

I teach Parts of Speech in the First Form, and I make no apology for it. (An English teacher)

An act of continuing faith is required in Grammar teaching. (English syllabus)

Why should a teacher be expected to apologize for including something in the syllabus if she could justify its inclusion on sound intellectual and educational grounds? But Parts of Speech occupy a special place in the mythology of English teaching, probably for no better reason than that old grammars, as far back as Greek grammars, *began* with a list of Parts of Speech. This mythology affirms several different kinds of belief. One is that Parts of Speech somehow represent the whole of Grammar. Another is that it is not possible to learn to write without knowing the Parts of Speech. Yet another is that it is possible to teach Parts of Speech by means of definitions that do not hold water. A fourth (common among secondary teachers) is that Parts of Speech are not taught in Primary Schools, and that therefore one should begin the pupils' secondary school careers by filling this gap in their education.

Most of these beliefs are present in the undertow of this English syllabus:

YEAR 1
Formal — Developments of Skills
1. Grammar: (a) parts of speech: nouns, verbs, adjectives, adverbs,
          (b) sentence — structure: statements, questions, commands
          (c) tenses — present, perfect and imperfect; infinitives

YEAR 2 begins:
1. Grammar: (a) revision of parts of speech from Year 1, plus conjunctions and prepositions

YEAR 3:
1. Grammar: (a) revision of all parts of speech
and

YEAR 4:
1. Grammar: consolidation of previous years work.

(Since there is no apostrophe on 'years', it is impossible to tell whether what is being referred to is YEAR 3, or YEARS 1, 2 and 3.)

There *is* an argument for teaching Parts of Speech. It is this. If one is going to talk about language with one's pupils, then one will need a language in which to do the talking, some technical terms. The names of the Parts of Speech in English will be among those technical terms. Knowing and understanding them will not, of itself, necessarily lead to an improvement in one's ability to talk, or to write. Knowing them and understanding them will provide some part of a common language in which aspects of language use may be discussed.

The syllabus quoted above suggests that the school is not sure that its method of teaching them leads to knowledge and understanding. Otherwise, why do they (as with full stops and commas in many English syllabuses) have to be 'revised' in Year 3 and 'consolidated' in Year 4? Should it not be possible to teach them in such a way that, like learning to swim or learning to ride a bicycle, yearly revision becomes unnecessary?

A good discussion of why the usual method of teaching Parts of Speech does not succeed is to be found in Frank Palmer's *Grammar*.[12] He points out that the traditional definitions, such as 'A noun is the name of a person, place or thing' or 'A verb is a doing word', do not actually work unless you already know the answer. In a sentence like, 'Grandma had one of her queer turns yesterday', the answer to the question 'What is the verb?' must surely, by the usual definitions, be 'turns'. It is the only 'doing' word in the sentence. It is little wonder that generations of school-children, misled by unhelpful definitions like these, should have come through the system without fully understanding what words like 'noun' and 'verb' mean.

The only satisfactory way of teaching Parts of Speech, once you are sure *why* you want to teach them, is by exploring the way in which words actually function in sentences, that is, in a functional framework. One method of doing this has already been suggested in Unit D2 of *Language in Use*, quoted on page 52 – 3.

This method has several advantages. It makes use of the pupils' intuitive knowledge of the structure of English. They *know* which words can follow which, because they have learnt about word-order as they developed their capacity to make meaning in language.

It draws attention to the fact that there are two categories of Parts of Speech, here called 'content' words (nouns, adjectives, verbs, adverbs and pronouns) and 'form' words (prepositions and conjunctions). (Frequently, in course books, the interjection ('Gosh') is added to make the 'Eight Parts of Speech', which are listed without any functional distinction being drawn.)

It can be used to explore such features of the language as the fact that nouns are often collocated with words like 'the', 'a' (or 'an'), 'that' and 'their', but that such words are frequently separated from the noun by one or more adjectives. The behaviour of verbs, and how they can be built up into verbal groups like, 'The class was *going to be kept in* after school', can also be explored in this way.

Another method of focusing attention on the function of Parts of Speech in sentences is by means of an adaptation of Cloze procedure, that is by using as a basis for discussion passages from which nouns, or verbs, or whatever it is desired to concentrate on, have been omitted.

Insights gained from explorations like this can then be invested it what may look like the traditional exercises of the course-books, but which are in fact significantly different. They are designed to enable pupils to make use of knowledge which pupils have made explicit to themselves in further exploration. Thus, a challenge to complete this sentence, or that, with an appropriate noun requires understanding of how the structure works both grammatically and semantically: a functional framework is provided.

A note on dialect

West Indians have a particular difficulty with tenses and word endings.
(English syllabus)

What did the writer of this sentence really mean? That West Indians are unable to talk about past and future time, or that they are unable to distinguish between singular and plural if the distinction rests upon the word endings? Almost certainly not. What she was complaining about was the seeming inability of her West Indian pupils to use the grammatical forms appropriate to Standard English where it is seen to matter — in writing. This is a linguistic problem not peculiar to West Indian children. It is, and always has been, shared, although not always to the same degree, by all native *speakers* of an English dialect other than Standard who find themselves having to *write* in standard. What can be done to help them?

The first essential, as always, is to understand the nature of their problem. Here they are, already possessing a fully functioning linguistic system, needing to acquire alternative forms if they are to succeed in the educational system, that is, if they are to acquire the ability to write in a way that will satisfy their teachers and examiners.

It may be argued, as, for example, Peter Trudgill argues in *Accent, Dialect and the School*,[13] that it should not be necessary to have to do this, that, so long as what is written is meaningful, then the linguistic form of expression used to convey the meaning should be acceptable. But, as Trudgill concedes, in the real world in which we live it is not possible to adopt this attitude. The expectations of the readers who finally matter dictate otherwise.

The second essential is to go about things in the right way. This means, above all, not starting from the position that the grammar and vocabulary of dialects are wrong, something, as one teacher declared, to be 'rooted out' at all costs.

The differences between the pupil's language, thus criticized, and the teacher's is likely to be minimal, compared with the amount of language that they have in common. Martin Joos, the author of *The Five Clocks*, commented vigorously on the undue attention concentrated on linguistic differences, as opposed to similarities, in the article called 'Language and the School Child' that he contributed to the Harvard Educational Review in 1964:

> When a child is said to speak 'ungrammatically' the fact is always that he is obeying a vast number of grammatical rules, a very small fraction of which happen to be different grammar rules from the ones that the critic subscribes to. The critic does not notice . . . that the child is obeying any rules at all. For that vast majority in which there is identity between the child's grammar and the critic's grammar, the critic notices no rules because there is no conflict; in that small minority of all the rules

57

for which there is conflict instead of identity, the critic notices only the conflict and does not recognize that the child's pattern has its own logic and is part of a different grammar just as rigid as the critic's own.[14]

The attitude which says that where these language differences exist they must be 'rooted out' is tantamount to saying that the language from which such items have to be 'rooted out' is an inferior kind of language, which must be replanted, or recolonized, by a superior kind. It is a small step from devaluing someone's language in this way to devaluing the person himself. This, in turn, is reflected in the person's self-image, with consequences that, for pupils in school, can be disastrous. It is well known that pupils' perceptions of themselves as pupils have an important bearing on their willingness to want to learn. If they are made to feel, from the outset, that their main channel of learning, their language, is inadequate for the purpose, then it is not surprising that they give up the endeavour and, instead, devote their energies to devising survival strategies outside the main stream of the school's activities, even to the extent of deliberately refusing to use linguistic forms regarded by the teacher as appropriate.

The starting point must be with the language of the pupil; it cannot be elsewhere. (It should be emphasized again that we are here concerned with pupils who speak as their mother-tongue a dialect of English, whether their origins are from within or outside England itself.) But what they possess is not only the linguistic system which gives them the linguistic potential to make meaning, but also a well developed body of intuitions about the way in which language functions. Among these is the perception that language involves an element of choice: we have a choice of what to say, or write, and how to say, or write, it.

Choice, like language itself, operates at different levels. At some levels, so habitual is our way of saying things, it is as if the choice is made for us. This applies, for example, to our vowels, to our use of glottal stops, and to other features of what is called our 'pronunciation'. It also applies to our use of various grammatical features, and to those distinctive items of vocabulary which belong to each dialect.

But most of us know that ours is not the only way of saying things. We can hear the differences between the ways in which people speak as we listen to them talking. In fact, we can go further than that. We think, as we listen to someone speaking, 'Oh, yes, he comes from Tyneside, he's a Geordie.' 'She comes from Liverpool'. 'He's a West Indian.' 'She's from India or Pakistan.' We can recognize the differences, even though we may not be able to describe them linguistically in the way in which Hughes and Trudgill describe them in *English Accents and Dialects*.

Children are very good at recognizing these differences, and at mimicking the accents of others. They are also surprisingly good at identifying, explicitly, particular points of difference. This ability, and the knowledge on which it rests, can be put to good use.

Out of the rapidly growing number of published examples that attest that this is indeed the case, here are two.

ILEA's Local English Centre situated in Vauxhall Manor School, in London, produced, between 1976 and 1979, a series of papers under the general heading 'Looking at Language'. One of them, 'Jennifer and Brixton Blues', is the text of a play written by two West Indian girls, Jennifer and Marcia. In his commentary on the text, John Richmond has this to say about Jennifer's ability to adjust her speech according to her perception of the audience:

> Thus, Jennifer uses 'Me' as the subject pronoun throughout most of the play, and particularly in conversation with peers. However, in two public situations, the church and her interchange with the rentman, she changes to 'I' (or 'A' as it has been spelt in the second case). This is not an accident, the product of disorganization and lack of good grammar, but a subtle, probably unconscious, adjustment of form to suit a different audience. The church demands respectability of manner, the creditor rentman has to be placated. Another example: the simple negative ('me nuh know', 'no want something drink?') is used throughout the play. However, in conversation with the white neighbour who is borrowing sugar, Jennifer's phrase is 'You don't need to bring it back Okay?' and 'I'm having a party tonight and I hope the noise don't bother you', (the latter using a feature of another, this time white, non-standard dialect). The form of her speech is immediately adjustable to audience and occasion.[15]

In the third number of The English Magazine, produced by the English Centre of the Inner London Education Authority, there is an article by David Halligan called 'Working together on Language'.[16] It is an account of the way in which a group of third-year pupils first of all discussed dialects, and their use of them, and then put their insights to use in a piece of work. At one point in the article, Halligan comments,

Situation, then, was seen by the girls to be the main factor influencing the way that they spoke. The following extracts from their talk show them defining it in terms of who the speakers are, what their relationship is, and why they have come together.

Jill: If you're going for an interview, right . . .

Sola: If you're going for a job you want a man to get a good impression, right, so you talk . . .

Tracey: Very nicely.

Jill: And you don't talk Cockney or have chewing bubble gum in your mouth.

Jill: I like using my voice sometimes. You know when you're at home, right, and you're with your friends, right, just talking natural . . .

Tracey: Yea, when you're at home and you want to put a good impression in front of your mum and your friends, you talk all nicely. It's when you get outside and you . . .

Marlene: Yea, it's when you get outside and you start talking your Cockney rebel and your Jamaican and all the rest of it.

Tracey: Yea, you talk different with your friends . . .

Jill: Listen Jenny, say there was six or seven of us, right, sitting round a table all talking naturally, right, and you come out and you said something, right, about, 'Oo, my mummy's got a big car,' or all that lot. What d'you think we're gonna do, bloody sit there and listen to a snob?

The girls did not necessarily see any justification for the attitude to Cockney expressed in the first extract, but they were clearly well aware of other people's attitudes. So important is situation that one girl had been very embarrassed by an incident in which the person she had been speaking to did not play the dialect game according to the rules.

Jill: When I first met my uncle's girlfriend, I thought she was really nice. She is nice but she's, er, she's common, you know what I mean, and she really is nice. I was talking really, really nice saying, 'Do you like jam?' and all this lot and she's going, 'Yea, course I do,' so I felt really shamed up.

Sola:	Embarrassed?
Jill:	Yea.
Tracey:	'Cos you were talking nicely and there's her . . .
Jill:	She was talking naturally, and I was talking poshly to her.

The group was then asked to produce different descriptions of an incident, a street fight. The group decided to produce the first version in London West Indian, the second in Cockney, and the third as it might be given to a policeman in Standard. There then follows a description of how the group went about the task, and of the insights that they brought to their task.

This is not without its problems. To produce the best version they needed to use the expertise in the group, but at the same time, to maintain the relationships in the group they had to see that everyone was involved. However, when they had finished the three versions and I had listened to the tape of them working, I was unsure whether they really thought that someone in this situation would use 'Jamaican' to friends and Cockney to mother. Had they really decided to do this in order to give everyone a job rather than to tackle the issue of the sort of dialect switching that happens in the real world? To get them to probe this issue I asked them to talk about the reasoning behind the versions that they had produced. It became clear that both explanations were true in part. They had done it that way to involve all of the group, but at the same time the West Indian girls did speak more 'Jamaican' with their friends than at home. As Marlene had already said, '. . . it's when you get outside and you start talking your Cockney rebel and your Jamaican and all the rest of it.' If the desire to collaborate had produced a distortion in the interests of maintaining the relationships in the group, it was really to polarize the dialect differences in the situation by suggesting that dialect choices are of an either/or sort rather than being made form a continuum. The subsequent discussion showed the girls' awareness of this.

Marlene:	When you're talking to your mum sometimes you tend to go off a bit, talk a little bit of Jamaican and a little bit of Cockney and at the same time . . .
Jenny:	When you get excited . . .
Marlene:	Yea, that's what happens.
Jackie:	You get carried away.
Jenny:	So that you're expressing something to your mum.

There was, however, no doubt about the rightness of Standard when giving an account of the incident to a policeman. One of the girls said, 'You wouldn't go and talk Cockney to a policeman, or Jamaican, now would you? . . . You have to give the police a good impression of you, because if you talk Cockney, he'll think you're lying.' When the power differences between speakers are as great as this it seems the status of Standard verges upon the moral.

These pupils obviously had a clear understanding of the fact that language varies according to the context in which language occurs and according to what it is being used for. In other words, they understand the linguist's concept of *register*. Writing is a register. Once pupils have got as far as understanding this, the recognition that the language used must relate to the register should follow. Choosing the appropriate forms is the final step.

Where necessary, detailed explanatory work may be done on grammatical differences, of the kind that is already often done on lexical differences, such as collecting the words that are used in different parts of the country for the same thing (e.g. bread) or for the same quality (e.g. being left-handed). In classes like those to be found in our big cities, containing speakers of a number of different dialects, it should be possible to take some of the features listed by Hughes and Trudgill in Chapter 2 of their book, for example, present and past tense forms, and see how many occur in the speech of its members, with the teacher ensuring that the standard English form is included. In the event of its not being used by any pupil in the class, it will almost certainly be known to them. Apart from featuring in their reading, radio and television have ensured that there is now widespread acquaintance with a rich diversity of accents and dialects.

As we know, such acquaintance with will not lead automatically to use of. It is one thing to hear, and recognize, the forms of Standard English on the lips of others, or to see and understand them in print. It is quite another to incorporate them into one's own speech — or writing. In order to do so, three conditions must be fulfilled: one must recognize the necessity; one must want to do it; and one must have the linguistic means at one's disposal.

There is now substantial evidence that, when a context is provided for pupils in which these conditions have been fulfilled, encouraging results can be obtained. Programmes of work have been devised in which pupils have to write different accounts of a happening, ranging from an entry in a diary, in which the language used is of concern only to the writer, to a formal report which has to be written in a precise form and a prescribed style. Stories in which the narrative is in Standard and the dialogue in dialect are also very productive. Where the concepts of register and audience are already well understood, the point is readily taken and motivation seems to follow.

It is not, of course, a question of doing something like this as a one-off exercise in the fourth or fifth years, as an exam at 16-plus looms ahead. Rather, the five statutory years of secondary education should see a gradual, and cumulative, increase in the potential of choice available to pupils. Indeed, the process should begin in primary schools, once they have begun to add to their linguistic repertoire the power of choosing to write.

7 Implications

There is another breakthrough still to come, in the training of teachers, who have so far been left to fend for themselves as far as language is concerned. Perhaps we may look forward to a time when language study has some place in the professional training of all teachers . . .   (M.A.K. Halliday, 1974[1])

A substantial course on language in education (including reading) should be part of every primary and secondary school teacher's initial training . . .   (*A Language for Life*, 1975[2])

Both quotations have already been used in the course of the attempt made to answer the question, 'How can we help pupils in our schools to write better?' One clear implication of the position argued in the book, that we can do more than we currently seem able, is that teachers are not given the intellectual equipment necessary to do the job. Despite the massive additions to our knowledge of language made by linguists over the last decades, very little has percolated through to the classroom to make the teaching more effective. Even now, five years after the Bullock Report called for a 'substantial course on language . . .' to be included in the training of every teacher, only a small proportion of students in training are involved in any worthwhile linguistically based study of language. This applies to teachers in general, and, regrettably, to English teachers in particular.

It may, perhaps, be necessary, at this point, to make explicit the view of English teaching, and thus of the English teacher's job, that underlies that expression of regret.

English teaching is about language, about the part played by language in the lives and learning of the pupils, and about helping pupils to develop their ability to use their own language. From this it follows that knowledge of and about language[3] must form part of the English teacher's equipment for the job. It is central to his concerns.

However, even if we could, by some means, ensure that from the beginning of the next academic year *all* teachers in training could have a course of language study, there remains a question to be answered. What exactly do teachers, in their role as teachers, need to know about language? Perhaps it would be better to ask, What do teachers need to understand about language? Knowledge, of itself, might not be enough. Language study courses seeking merely to pass on a body of linguistic knowledge to the students do not necessarily influence the practice of teachers in the classroom. Knowledge must be accompanied by understanding of how language is working in the lives of the pupils while they are in school. This book has suggested some of the key areas in which such knowledge and understanding are necessary.

1. Early language learning. How and why do we acquire the ability to speak? The functional basis of language.
2. The individual and his language; the nature of spoken language; dialect and accent.
3. Writing systems, and their relationship to speech. The English writing system.
4. Language and choice. What options are available to a language-user?

It is not as if nothing has been written about these matters. The series to which this book is a contribution was designed to bring linguistic insights to the attention of teachers. The first volume, *Language Study, the Teacher and the Learner*, discussed the whole concept of Language Study in relation to the needs of both teachers and learners, and provided a guide to the reading that was available when it was published in 1973. Since then, we have had M.A.K. Halliday on early language learning in *Learning How to Mean* and on the functional basis of language in *Explorations in the Functions of Language*; Roger Gurney on the biological basis of language in *Language, Brain and Interactive Processes*; Peter Trudgill on accent and dialect in *Accent, Dialect and the School*; and the language of the home and the language of school in the Doughty's *Language and Community* and my own *Language, Experience and School*.

The series itself stemmed from the work of the Schools Council Programme in Linguistics and English Teaching, from *Language in Use*, and from *Exploring Language*, the book which made explicit the linguistic theory which informed *Language in Use*. Other recent and relevant books have been quoted, or referred to, in the text.

Another clear implication of the position argued in the book is that, if we are to do more for our pupils, changes will have to be made in the way in which classrooms are organized, in which 'marking' is done, in which school examinations in English are set, in which school reports are written, and in which schools explain themselves to parents, governors and other interested outside bodies.

Much has been made of the need to allow pupils to talk together, to discuss assignments, to collaborate in drafting pieces of writing. The difference between a classroom organized to permit this, and one in which heads are obediently bent over course-books, is very wide. The former requires teachers who are confident in what they are doing because they understand its rationale. Pupils need to be educated into the techniques. Higher authority in the school needs to understand what is going on, and why. Marking for 'correctness' will be replaced by a more sensitive indication of 'problems', with the offer of help always implied. This will need to be explained to parents, especially those who expect every piece of written work to be religiously marked. End of year English examinations will no longer contain language exercises, to give a 'solid' content. (It is curious how, in the search for a spurious 'objectivity', teachers will resort to various kinds of test. It is interesting to note what a Primary School Headmaster wrote when he was asked to collect from his fourth-year pupils some written work that had been done as part of a project looking at the range of written work done in the ordinary course of school-work. 'Although standardized data on reading skills, grammar, punctuation and spelling, and IQ was available for all children in the fourth-year group, none of these factors appeared to have high correlation with the children's written work.') The tradition of Mode 3 has now been well established in CSE, and is beginning to penetrate O level. Has not the time come to use Mode 3-type assessment in English from the first forms upward? If, from their output for the year, pupils themselves are asked to nominate, say, fifteen pieces on which their yearly assessment will be made, they will, perhaps, be motivated to produce finished products and to exercise judgment. In any case, a file of finished products is more encouraging than an exercise book in which red ink records, from page 1, that no progress is being made. Allowing the English Department to submit Mode 3 assessments may mean exempting it from the school's examination procedure. This, in turn, may spell difficulty.

School reports characteristically contain remarks like 'His spelling is appalling', 'Her spelling remains weak', or 'Spelling is holding him back'. The answer to such reports, for the parent who is concerned, is a one-word question, 'Why?', followed by another question, 'What are you doing to improve matters?' Once parents understand that their children's spelling is susceptible of improvement, then schools will be under an obligation to bring it about. This may have the effect of breaking open the situation into which teachers and parents find themselve locked. Teachers continue to use methods that do not work. Parents see that the desired result (e.g. improved spelling) is not being produced, and suppose that this is either because insufficient attention is being paid to it, or because the methods that they remember from their own school days are no longer in use. Hence the cry, 'Back to Basics'. As James Moffett said, in the article already quoted, 'Where else have we ever *been*?' But teaching them ineffectively. Teachers have, on the whole, allowed the 'Back to Basics' debate to be conducted on the issue of teaching methods. If teaching methods currently in use were patently more effective, then 'back to basics', like any other discussion of curriculum, would be a debate about aims and objectives, with the question of methods being left to the professionals, i.e. the teachers. Statements of aims and objectives should never be confused with discussion of how to achieve them.

There are also important implications for the way in which English Departments are organized, and for the use that they make of resources. Emphasis has been placed, again and again, on the needs of the individual. This is inescapable. We learn individually, for ourselves. From time to time, we need individual help. The English, and Remedial, Departments must therefore be organized in a such a way as to permit the possibility of a pupil having individual attention and help. It can be done, as the withdrawal system in use in schools already demonstrates. Block time-tabling can enable one teacher to devote his or her time to a small group, and the individuals within it. Some schools make use of parents and senior pupils to provide, under the direction of the Head of Remedial, the same kind of tuition provided by Volunteer Tutors working in the Adult Literacy Scheme under the direction of professional coordinators, while in others members of both English and Remedial departments are time-tabled to provide a 'surgery' service during the lunch-hour for any pupil who cares to come for help.

Provision of individual learning opportunities on any scale requires an adequate supply of relevant teaching materials. Instead of relying on books which purport through exercises of the traditional kind to 'give pupils skills' in spelling, punctuation and sentence construction (publishers' lists remain full of them — if they work, why do we need so many?), English and Remedial Departments will have to make collections of learning strategies aimed at the actual needs of individuals, building up a repertoire of ideas that have brought success to somebody. They will, in addition, require space within the school, not only physical space, but time-table space.

It may be objected that bringing all this about will disturb existing organizational patterns in schools. However, if we are agreed about the aim, then it follows that we should seek to achieve that aim through methods that give promise of success. That methods currently in use do not bring success is incontrovertible. Why have we been so slow to abandon them, even if it meant making major changes to the way in which schools are run? Posed like this, it is clear that the question is a fundamental one about the secondary school curriculum.

In John F. Kerr's contribution to *The Curriculum: Context, Design & Development*, the curriculum is defined as, all the learning which is planned and guided by the school, whether it is carried on in groups or individually, inside or outside the school.'[4] The curriculum is, in short, that which the school intends. It is the sum total of the way in which the school organizes experiences, allocates resources and makes use of its agents in order to achieve its expressed purposes. Among these, surely, making pupils literate must rank very highly. How, when they fail to accomplish this among their purposes do schools manage to explain it away? The answer lies deep in the structure of the education system, in the way in which that structure reflects what is seen as the purpose of education, and in the view that is taken of the educability of pupils. A widow of eighty-seven, who learnt through the Adult Literacy Scheme to write to her grandchildren in Australia, demonstrated that there is virtually no age beyond which people cease to be educable. We need to be very careful before writing off pupils because we say we cannot teach them.

If we are in earnest about giving pupils genuine chances in comprehensive schools, then we must be in earnest about giving them help with their learning. This book has explored the implications of this proposition, as far as writing is concerned, for teachers, for the schools in which they teach, and for those who train them for teaching. There are implications, too, for those on the periphery of education — politicians, professors, publishers, and those who write on education in the press. They might start to think their way through to an intellectually respectable position, from which they could make contributions to discussion designed to assist, rather than hinder, the cause of educating our young. We might then look forward to a world in which professors of English did not express their 'distress' that formal grammar was not being taught, while pupils in schools were being held back because formal grammar still formed the basis of what was being taught.

Meanwhile, it is always open to those who do not accept the argument of the book to demonstrate, by the success of their own methods, where it is inadequate.

Appendix
A BASIC OUTLINE FOR WORKING WITH GROUPS
Peter Doughty

1. A THEME which relates to everyone is introduced, rehearsed informally by the teacher.
2. It is then explored through TEACHER ELICITED RESPONSE (to give class time to gain familiarity with the implications of the THEME).
3. THEME is then explored in small working groups (pairs in the same desk provide the limiting case).

   The pre-conditions for the move to 3 are:
   - (i)   rapport established between teacher and class,
   - (ii)   class in possession of some basic cohesion,
   - (iii)   elicited response to THEME has been positive.

   Direction is given by the request for a report to the whole class: lead questions are provided.

   (During 3 teacher functions as entrepreneur, consultant and organizer of the action.)
4. The reports from the groups: the form is a forum discussion, but the work on the THEME should have put everyone in a position to participate (the key aspects of the THEME have been rehearsed verbally).

   Teacher now adopts the role of questioning chairman (notes key issues, relates response of one group to that of another).

   Extent of 4 will depend on the level of interest shown.

   Variant of 4 with older pupils experienced in work of this kind: student-directed forum discussion (teacher absent: tape used to record session).
5. Teacher puts his summing up of the explorations, and builds in anything that has been left out. Basically EXPOSITION (but with continuous reference to what has been done).
5. Variants: (a)   A summing-up and rounding off at the end

of a run, preparatory to the taking up of some quite different direction.

(b) A summing up as a basis for a new development of the original direction.

(c) A recapitulation of what has been done so far, to give continuity and maintain direction, where the topic is being pursued over an extended period of time.

(b) and (c) show the 'recursive' element in group work, for they are another form of 1. and so the cycle can be worked through again.

6. Relating work tasks to this process.

(i) They can be *teacher* directed, but student-oriented — a common subject aimed at experience all pupils can be expected to possess, in relation to the topic.

(ii) They can be *theme* directed: written work which arises out of the exploration itself (a crucial factor here is that the writing involves material that has been talked through). Work of this kind is often 'informational'.

(iii) They can be *theme* related: the progress of the exploration gives rise to questions which can be taken up personally by individual pupils, and yet remain within the orbit of the work.

(No Groups can discuss 'literature' as part of their experience of 'English': the teacher could ask for an assignment in which a pupil talked about a book that had meant a great deal.)

(iv) They can be the choice of the pupil, guided by the frame of the theme:

(a) selected from a short list the class itself can construct,

(b) selected individually.

References

Chapter 1   Introductory
1   Education in Cheshire, Summer 1977.
2   Shaughnessy, Mina P. *Errors and Expectations*, p. 3 (OUP, 1977 ISBN 019 502 137 6)
3   (Ed) Clegg, A. B. *The Excitement of Writing*, p. xi (Chatto & Windus, 1967)
4   See, for example
    Britton, J. *et al. The Development of Writing Abilities (11 – 18)* (Macmillan, 1975 ISBN 333 17862 9)
    Burgess, C. *et al. Understanding Children Writing* (Penguin, 1973 ISBN 0 1408 0700 4)
    Martin, N. *et al. Writing and Learning across the Curriculum* (Ward Lock, 1976 ISBN 0 7062 3498 7)
    Medway, P. *From Talking to Writing* (Ward Lock, 1976 ISBN 0 7062 3565 7)
    Martin, N. *et al. Why Write?* (Ward Lock, 1976 ISBN 0 7062 3566 5)
    See also
    A Language for Life (The Bullock Report) Chapter 11, Written Language (HMSO, 1975 ISBN 0 11 270326 7)
5   Harpin, W. R. *The Second 'R'*, p. 157 (Unwin, 1976 ISBN 0 04 372019 6)

Chapter 2   Language in our heads
1   Cazden, C. B. *Child Language and Education*, p. 3 (Holt, Rinehart and Winston, ISBN 0 03 077130)
2   Halliday, M.A.K. *Language and Social Man*, p. 27 'Children grow up, and their language grows with them. By the age of

two and a half or even earlier, the child has mastered the adult language *system*; the framework is all there. He will spend the rest of his childhood — the rest of his life, even — mastering the adult *language*.'
(Originally published in the Second Series of Papers in Linguistics from the Schools Council Programme in Linguistics and English Teaching, Longman, 1974. Reprinted in *Language as Social Semiotic*, Edward Arnold, 1978-ISBN 07131 5967 7)

3   Abercrombie, D. *Studies in Phonetics and Linguistics*, p. 43. See also chapters 7 and 8. (OUP, 1965)
4   Sartre, J. *Les Mots* (Gallimard, 1964) Published in translation as *Words* (Penguin, 1967 ISBN 14 002727 0) p. 104
5   Hughes, A. and Trudgill, P. *English Accents and Dialects*, p. 8 (Edward Arnold, 1979 ISBN 0 7131 6129 9)
6   Hughes and Trudgill, *op cit* p. 14
7   Labov, W. 'The logic of non-standard English', reprinted in (Ed) Keddie, N. *Tinker, Tailor* (Penguin, 1973 ISBN 0 14 080381 5)

Chapter 3   Behaviour on Paper

1   Young, J.Z. *Programs of the Brain*, p. 189 (OUP, 1978 ISBN 0 19 857545 9)
2   Britton, J. *et al. op cit* p. 47
3   Shaughnessy, Mina P. *op cit*, p. 12

Chapter 4   'Some such rot'

1   Forster, E. M. *Marianne Thornton*, pp. 233 – 4 (Edward Arnold, 1956)
2   Wilkinson, A. *The Foundations of Language*, pp. 32 – 5 (OUP, 1971 ISBN 0 19 911016 6)
3   Mountain, A. B. & Barnes, W. *Effective English*, Book 4 (Schofield & Sims, 1961)
4   Harris, R. J. 'The Only Disturbing Feature. . . .' (The Use of English, 1963)
5   *A Language for Life*, pp. 227, 8
6   Halliday, M.A.K. *Language and Social Man*, original version, p. 66
7   Moffett, J. 'Language Learning in the Eighties', in McGill Journal of Education, Winter 1979, p. 103

8   Thompson, D. in *The Excitement of Writing*, pp. ix, x
9   *Aspects of secondary education in England*, Chapter 6, Language (HMSO, 1979 ISBN 0 11 270498 0)

Chapter 5   Writing in school

1   *Letter to a Teacher* by the School of Barbiana, p. 25 (Penguin, 1970)
2   *Aspects of secondary education in England*, p. 102
3   *Writing for an Audience* (ILEA Learning Materials Service, Highbury Station Rd., London, N1 1SB)
4   Martin, N. *Here, Now and Beyond*, pp. 206 – 10 (OUP, 1968 ISBN 019 833144 4)
5   Halliday, M.A.K. 'Differences between Spoken and Written Language' (unpublished mimeo)

6   Fines, J. and Verrier, R. *The Drama of History*, pp. 81 – 4 (New University Education, 1974 ISBN 0 05157 512 9)
7   See
     Pearce, J. *et al. People in Touch* (Edward Arnold, 1978 ISBN 0 7131 0223 3)
     Pearce, J. *et al. Hold the Line* (Edward Arnold, 1979 0 7131 0358 2)
     Daniels, M. *There's a Lot of Language about* (McGraw Hill, 1979 ISBN 0 07 084244 2)
     Doughty, A. & P. *Using 'Language in Use'* (Edward Arnold, 1974 ISBN 0 7131 1897 0)
8   *A Language for Life*, Principal Recommendation 4, p. 514

Chapter 6   Relevant and effective help

1   Moorhouse, C. *Helping Adults to Spell*, p. 15 (Interprint Graphic Services Ltd., Half Moon St., Bagshot, Surrey)
2   Torbe, M. *Teaching Spelling*, p. 18 (Ward Lock, 1977 ISBN 0 7062 3663 7)
3   See
     Keen, J. *Teaching English — a linguistic perspective*, Chapter 3 (Methuen, 1978 ISBN 0 416 7082 X)
4   See, for example,
     (Ed) Browne, Y. *Hard Words — helping pupils to spell* (ILEA English Centre, Sutherland St., London, SW1)
     In a Word (Macmillan, in association with ILEA)

BBC Writing and Spelling Handbook (BBC, 1979 ISBN 0 563 16292 9)

5   Keen, J. *op cit*, Chapter 2, Understanding your students' language
For other examples of how to see childrens' writing as evidence see Richmond, J. *Progress in Pat's Writing* (Looking at Language, The Vauxhall Manor Papers, Local Centre for English, Lambeth Teachers' Centre, Santley St., London SW4)
Binns, R. *From Speech to Writing* (SCDS, Moray House College, Edinburgh)
Open University Language Development Course, PE 232 — Language Development Block 6, Supplementary Readings (SUP 05 11 79), *Comments on secondary writing*, p. 86 et seq

6   Mackay, D. *et al.* Breakthrough to Literacy — Teachers' Manual, pp. 73 – 6, 123 – 149 (Rev. edn. Longman, 1978 ISBN 0 582 19134 3)

7   Albrow, K. H. *The English Writing System* (Papers in Linguistics, Longman, 1972)

8   Halliday, M.A.K. 'Differences between Spoken and Written Language'

9   Palmer, F. *Grammar*, p. 71, but see the whole of chapters 1 and 2 (Penguin 1971, ISBN 0 14 02 1333 3)

10 Crystal, D. *Child Language, Learning and Linguistics*, p. 66 (Edward Arnold, 1976 ISBN 0 7131 5891 3)

11 Doughty *et al. Language in Use*, Unit D2, p. 93 (Edward Arnold, 1971 ISBN 0 7131 1679 X)

12 Palmer, F. *op cit*, Chapter 2.

13 Trudgill, P. *Accent, Dialect and the School*, Chapter 4, p. 80 (Edward Arnold, in this series, 1975 ISBN 0 7131 1983 7)
See also
Richmond, J. 'Dialect in the Classroom', in The English Magazine, No. 2 (ILEA English Centre)

14 Joos, M. 'Language and the School Child', in Harvard Educational Review, 1964

15 (Ed) Richmond, J. *Jennifer and Brixton Blues* (Looking at Language, The Vauxhall Manor Papers)

16 Halligan, D. 'Working together on Language', in the English Magazine, No. 3 (ILEA English Centre)

Chapter 7   Implications

1   Halliday M.A.K. 'Language and Social Man', p. 66

2 *A Language for Life*, p. 515
3 For this distinction, see
Doughty, P. *et al. Exploring Language*, p. 21 – 3 (Edward Arnold, 1972 ISBN 0 1716 8)
4 Kerr, John F. 'The problem of curriculum reform', in (ed) Hooper, R. *The Curriculum: Context, Design & Development* (Oliver & Boyd, in association with The Open University Press, 1971 ISBN 0 05 002464 7), p. 181

Further reading

For those wishing to explore some of the issues raised in the book in more detail, Mina Shaughnessy's *Errors and Expectations* is required reading. Bibliographical details will be found in the references to Chapter 1, p. 72.

On aspects of the linguistic background, see Crystal, D. *Child Language, Learning and Linguistics* (details on p. 75), Palmer, F. *Grammar* (p. 75), Hughes, A. and Trudgill, P. *English Accents and Dialects* (p. 73), Trudgill, P. *Accent, Dialect and the School* (p. 75).

For works on aspects of the writing system (spelling, punctuation, etc) see the references to Chapter 6 (p. 74), together with Katherine Perera's chapter, 'Reading and Writing' in Cruttender, A. *Language in infancy and childhood* (Manchester University Press, 1979 ISBN 0 7190 0750) and Stubbs, M. *Language and Literacy* (Routledge and Kegan Paul, 1980, ISBN 0 7100 0499 0), especially Chapter 3.

Two forthcoming books will also be helpful:

Gannon, P. and Czerniewska, P. *Using Linguistics: an Educational Focus* (Edward Arnold, 1980) ISBN 0 7131 6294 5. See especially Chapter 4 — Children's writing — a linguistic comment.

Keen, J. *English Writing Skills* (Methuen, 1981). This is designed to give students 'a greater awareness of the choice of language open to them, and a greater awareness of the appropriateness of the alternatives.'